LACE

FROM THE
VICTORIA AND ALBERT MUSEUM

LACE

FROM THE
VICTORIA AND ALBERT MUSEUM

CLARE BROWNE

PHOTOGRAPHY BY CHRISTINE SMITH

V & A PUBLICATIONS

First published by V&A Publications, 2004
V&A Publications
160 Brompton Road
London SW3 1HW

© The Board of Trustees of the Victoria and Albert
Museum 2004

Clare Browne asserts her moral right to be identified
as the author of this book

Designed by Area
Photography by Christine Smith of the
V&A Photographic Studio

ISBN 1 85177 418 1

A catalogue record for this book is available from the
British Library

Front jacket illustration: Austrian needle-lace collar,
1880 (plate 87)
Back jacket illustrations, clockwise from top: Italian
bobbin lace, late 17th century (plate 28); Italian silk
needle lace, 1670–1700 (plate 27); Genoese bobbin
lace, 1630–40 (plate 15); Italian needle lace, 1620–40
(plate 10)
Frontispiece: Flemish needle lace, Brussels, 1750s
(plate 54)

Printed in Singapore

V&A Publications
160 Brompton Road
London SW3 1HW
www.vam.ac.uk

CONTENTS

FOREWORD

The lace collection at the Victoria and Albert Museum originated in a study collection of decorative arts assembled in the nineteenth century for the Government-run School of Design. The first acquisition of lace was made in 1847, a border of eighteenth-century Mechlin bobbin lace. The collection grew through purchase, gift and bequest and is now comprehensive in its scope, including lace from all the major lace-making centres in Europe, from the mid-sixteenth until the early twentieth century.

During the 1960s, '70s and '80s, the Museum's lace specialists were Patricia Wardle, then Santina Levey. Their judicious acquisitions and development of the V&A's collection, and their continuing outstanding scholarship in lace history, are gratefully acknowledged here.

Several criteria were used to select the 100 pieces to be illustrated from among so extensive a collection. Some pieces are included because they are exceptional or rare examples of their style and technique. Some, particularly nineteenth-century reproductions of historical styles, were chosen because their provenance enables them to be used as reference pieces. And some pieces are included as personal favourites.

INTRODUCTION

'Let it not be condemned for a superfluous wearing, because it doth neither hide nor heat, seeing it doth adorn.'
(Thomas Fuller, *The History of the Worthies of England*, 1662)

Over centuries we have used the term lace for textiles made in a variety of different techniques, with the common characteristic of an open, usually delicate structure, serving a purpose almost always decorative rather than practical. Thomas Fuller's comment underlines this perception. The term originally had the meaning of a narrow tape or braid, tie or cord, which we still recognize now. But by the late sixteenth century it was also being used as a descriptive term for all forms of openwork made with needle or bobbin.

Throughout its history this type of lace making has been a skill practised by both professionals and amateurs. The range of goods for which lace was used ran from the very top end of the fashionable market (pieces extravagantly costly and labour-intensive) down to simple home-made trimmings. High quality lace constantly changed both technically and stylistically in response to changes in fashion. These changes gradually had effect on lower quality, non-fashionable and domestic laces, allowing lace to be both a sensitive indicator of ephemeral fashions and a barely changing repository of historical styles.

❧ TECHNIQUE

Although the name has been applied to other techniques, all true hand-made lace belongs to one of two main technical groups, made either with the needle or with bobbins. The two techniques can in addition be combined in one piece of lace. The underlying processes used for needle lace and bobbin lace have remained the same from the late sixteenth century to the present day.

Needle lace is the term used for all forms of lace constructed stitch by stitch with needle and thread. Its origin is in cutwork, that is, needle lace based on a woven ground, from which areas have been cut away. *Reticella* was the sixteenth-century name given to geometric needle lace worked over the grid of threads left in a piece of linen after some threads had been withdrawn. Developing out of this, needle lace ceased to depend on a woven ground and came to be worked on a foundation of outlining threads laid over a parchment pattern, from which it was removed when completed. The lace was built up with rows of detached buttonhole stitches worked over the outlining threads, linked and elaborated in various ways.

Bobbin lace is the term used for all lace made by plaiting, twisting or weaving together a number of threads wound on small bobbins and secured at the ends to a hard pillow. The lace was worked over a pricked pattern originally of parchment, the threads kept in place during its construction with the use of pins. The earliest form of bobbin lace to develop was the type now known as straight lace, for which the complete piece of lace was made in one continuous process. Later, part lace was also developed, for which parts of the pattern were made separately and subsequently joined.

Fig. I
P.4–1974
Portrait of a Young Man,
by Nicholas Hilliard
English; about 1585–90
Watercolour on vellum
He is wearing a cutwork ruff.

EARLY BACKGROUND

These two forms of lace can both be dated in their origins to the late fifteenth and early sixteenth century. It was the manufacture of silk and metal braids to be laid down on the surface of rich materials (both for furnishing and for dress) that gave the impetus to the development of bobbin lace. In Italy, Milan was a centre for the production of *passementerie*, the ornaments and trimmings applied to furnishings, and Venice for a number of luxury textile trades, and both cities specialized in producing and working with the silk and metal thread from which much early bobbin lace was made. Different types of trimmings were produced working with bobbins, ranging from simple plaits to more complex braids and other constructions of silk and metal thread. Bobbin lace worked in these materials was applied to the surface of clothes and furnishings, and when worked in linen thread it was used as insertions and edgings for linen covers and garments.

The origins of needle lace lie in the increasingly visible use of white linen in fashionable dress and furnishings during the first half of the sixteenth century. In the fashion of this period, fine linen, although an important component, was visible only in certain areas, through slashed or open sleeves, filling in the fronts of low bodices, and at the neck and wrists. This restrained exposure stimulated its decoration with fine embroidery including whitework (white thread on white ground), elaborated with lines of openwork and cutwork. Decorated edges were given to the visible areas of shirts and smocks by cutting the linen into indentations, pulling or withdrawing threads on the inner side, and making tiny frills. Needle lace developed in the working of tiny detached edgings to the collars and cuffs, and in the fillings of cut-out holes and openwork grids of pulled-thread and drawn-thread areas. Seams were decorated by lacing together the edges of two pieces of material, or by attaching needle-made insertions, from simple loops to complex interlacings.

Gradually, during the second quarter of the sixteenth century, changing fashions in trimmings and embroidery resulted in the exaggeration of some effects, with greater emphasis being placed on decorated seams and edgings. Elaborate white embroidery and openwork became an increasingly important part of surface decoration, and needle and bobbin lace began to emerge more distinctly in response to these demands. However, needle and bobbin laces in the middle of the sixteenth century still differed in their general appearance, often in the materials of which they were made, and in the uses to which they were put. They came from different professional centres, and the two techniques became associated with different classes of society.

Flanders and Italy were the major centres for the early development of lace. The two regions produced both needle and bobbin lace, and lace production developed in both into a prestigious textile industry. There were strong commercial and cultural contacts between them and a flourishing trade. The dissemination of pattern books contributed to mutual stylistic and technical influence between the production centres.

The spread of pattern books had an important influence on the development of lace in the sixteenth century. German presses had been producing single pattern sheets for embroidery and lacis (darned net) from the late fifteenth century. Printed pattern books were produced in increasing numbers during the following century, with the contents gradually changing to include patterns for pulled thread, drawn thread and cutwork, and eventually lace patterns. They were usually produced in centres of printing and international trade rather than areas commercially important for embroidery and lace (for example, only one pattern book is known from Flanders), and were in most cases intended for amateur rather than professional needlewomen.

With very few exceptions, pattern books for embroidery and related techniques before the late sixteenth century did not include designs that could be used for bobbin lace, possibly because it was considered a household skill rather than an artistic accomplishment for fashionable ladies. Only two pattern books devoted entirely to bobbin-lace patterns are known to have been published in the sixteenth century, in Venice and Zurich. The Swiss work

8

suggested that the skill was introduced by Venetian merchants into Switzerland in 1536, initially as a cottage industry comparable to spinning, and used for trimming sheets and other household furnishings. The outlay on equipment for bobbin-lace making was minimal, and the value of the materials needed was low in comparison to the value of the end product. It was suited to providing cheap and productive employment in charitable institutions, and from the middle of the sixteenth century onwards records across Europe show the establishment of bobbin-lace making in orphanages, almshouses and prisons. The professional bobbin-lace makers worked to patterns provided by middlemen and linen merchants in direct response to the demands of their fashionable clients, their output based on steady sales to a dependable market.

During the third quarter of the sixteenth century there was a movement from white embroidery ornamented with drawn thread, pulled thread and cutwork towards more fully developed needle lace, although it was still dependent on a woven linen ground. Increasing areas of fabric were cut away to create a geometric grid of threads, over which the stitches were worked. This was cutwork in its most advanced form, which came to dominate fashion, reaching the height of technical and stylistic perfection around 1615 (plate 5). In the mid-sixteenth century it was being used to decorate collars, which developed into ruffs. There was a striking increase in the size of ruffs during the 1570s, and by 1580 these had become even larger and more elaborate. Wide, open ruffs were worn on a *supportasse* (wire frame), and the fashion developed to include wide flat collars supported on a frame, called standing collars or bands; it reached its peak about 1613.

Bobbin lace worked in linen thread was used in conjunction with needle lace in making the spiky edges of ruffs in the 1580s and '90s, and as cutwork became more open, bobbin lace began to be used as a cheaper alternative method of producing the same effect (plate 7). Bobbin-lace copies of cutwork were widely worn during the first thirty years of the seventeenth century, and brought the technique, worked in linen, into fashionable dress.

❧ THE SEVENTEENTH CENTURY

During the first quarter of the seventeenth century the link with a woven ground that underlay cutwork was broken, and lace moved on from being a trimming or surface decoration into a textile in its own right. The development was taken forward in Italy, where the taste for flowing patterns had led to the

development of *punto in aria*, the term used in this period for freely formed needle lace (plates 9 and 10). With the freedom from a geometrical structure that the technique allowed, surface pattern became more important.

Changes in men's and women's fashion in this period introduced a softer, more fluid style. These changes, which brought the wide standing collars down onto the shoulders and which finally ended the popularity of the ruff, were important to the development of lace. They originated in France, and the new style became common in England by the late 1620s. It gave more scope for the use of lace, and lace consumption rose enormously during the 1630s and '40s. Lace was displayed most ostentatiously on falling bands, but it was also used lavishly on every type of costume accessory, from boot-hose to caps, as well as on furnishings. Flemish bobbin lace, with its fine draping qualities, dominated the market. The Flemish industry had a skilled workforce and produced the finest linen thread. It was proficient at both following and anticipating the market, including the exacting demands of the French nobility, and benefited from its geographical position and contact with trade routes. Most Italian bobbin lace in this period was

9

Fig. 2
565–1882
Portrait of an Unknown Lady, possibly by Gilbert Jackson English; late 1620s
Oil on canvas
She is wearing a collar and cuffs of Flemish or English bobbin lace.

fairly heavy, used for furnishings, vestments, the trimming of heavy velvet clothes and large collars (plate 15). By contrast, Flemish bobbin lace was light and delicate, made with finer thread and more open patterns. In the age of cutwork it had been a cheaper option, but now its elaborate designs and fine threads made the best-quality pieces as expensive as Italian needle lace.

Flemish bobbin lace remained the major fashion lace until the 1660s. It held its position by undergoing a series of changes; from the 1630s onwards, the trade was able to produce whatever lace was applicable to the current fashion. The pot of flowers motif, particularly popular in that decade, was perfectly suited to the deep scallops that decorated falling bands. The size of scallops subsequently diminished, to become a straight edge by the mid-1650s. Wide falling bands were replaced in men's wear by bib-fronted bands, and for women by deep collars, which displayed perfectly the subtle patterns of Flemish bobbin lace (plate 20). The design of lace gradually changed, with single motifs replaced by series of sprigs or patterns of narrow swirling tapes. There was a parallel growth in this period of lace constructed with a tape-like base, both bobbin- and needle-made (plate 16). Black silk lace was also popular, and can be seen in many portraits, but very little has survived.

Lace patterns changed in line with Italian silk designs, and the need to find an unobtrusive background to the more open patterns of the 1650s and '60s led to the development of mesh-grounded laces (plate 21). The earliest were mostly of plaited threads, but regular meshes also developed, worked with the aid of pins. They were used in both straight laces, which are worked in one piece with the mesh therefore worked uniformly in one direction, and part laces, where the pattern pieces are worked separately and joined, and the mesh, worked to fit round them, has a continually varying direction.

Needle lace had continued to be made in Italy through the years of the mid-seventeenth century when Flemish bobbin lace dominated fashion. During the 1660s, under the influence of French fashion and the taste of Louis XIV and his court, Venetian needle lace took over as the most fashionable style. Venetian lace makers transformed needle lace into a three-dimensional fabric in keeping with the baroque style of the later seventeenth century, a style based on mass and movement, and bold motifs. The patronage of the Roman Catholic Church was also crucial to the rapid expansion of the industry. The Italian lace makers had elaborated the part-lace technique, so could split large baroque designs into sections, and produce large-scale items such as dress flounces, church vestments and furnishings (plate 22). They used a careful balance of solid form against space, with density broken up by filling stitches and flat surfaces relieved with three-dimensional detailing. The costume items on which Venetian lace was shown to best advantage were wide collars for women and bib-fronted bands for men (plate 23). These bands, displaying scrolling baroque designs in mirror image, were worn by men of fashion throughout Europe between 1660 and 1690. Venetian lace in all forms was widely worn at the English court. Legislation in 1662 had banned the importation and selling of foreign lace except by the king's own lace merchant, but nevertheless it continued to be freely sold and worn in London.

Boldly patterned three-dimensional lace remained popular until the end of the seventeenth century, but in Venice the technique was used for needle lace in a variety of scales, some of exceptional delicacy and elaboration (plates 24 and 25). All shared a common style of branching, curving stems with exotic leaves and flowers. A flat type of needle lace was also made in Venice, which probably developed in response to changes in fashionable dress and the success of French needle lace (plate 26).

Another important baroque lace was a type of bobbin lace usually attributed to Milan, although it may also have been made in Venice and Genoa. It had clear links with Venetian needle lace, visible in the use of cord outlines and the small three-dimensional motifs known in English as wheat-ears (plate 28). Milanese lace typically included pictorial motifs among baroque scrolls, and this style may have developed as a result of the patronage of the Church, being extensively used for altar linen and vestments. The technique was based on tapes worked in cloth stitch (plain weave made with bobbins), and fully developed mesh grounds were used in Milanese lace from at least the 1670s, as well as bars to link the motifs. Lace making of this type spread into other areas of Italy, Austria and the Slav countries and continued into the eighteenth century, so the attribution and dating of surviving pieces can be very difficult.

Towards the end of the seventeenth century Flemish bobbin lace was copying Milanese in its style, but it was softer in effect and more delicate. Like Milanese, it could be worked with a ground of either bars or mesh, the mesh sometimes elaborate (plate 30). By the 1690s it had become light and airy, influenced by French lace, and leaving the baroque style behind.

It was to stop the import of costly Venetian needle and Flemish bobbin laces that in 1665 the French government established state-sponsored industries to develop local needle and bobbin lace. Lace making did exist in France before this, with the oldest established industry in the Auvergne, on the main trade routes to Italy and Spain, and production in centres in the Paris area, and Normandy. Colbert, Louis XIV's Minister of Arts and Manufactures, induced Venetian and Flemish lace makers to come to France, and they were allocated to a number of towns selected as centres for the new industry. The most successful was the needle-lace industry based at Alençon and Argentan. French needle lace, known as *point de France*, soon began to compete with that of Venice, developing a distinctive form with patterns in the style of Jean Berain, Louis XIV's designer. These combined renaissance grotesques and strapwork with chinoiserie, in very detailed designs that had motifs of figures, animals, trophies and exotic motifs (plate 31). Since *point de France* was more delicate than most Venetian lace, it was better suited to the developing fashion for gathered cravats and flounces, and elaborate headdresses.

The taste of the French court in the later seventeenth century also favoured gold and silver bobbin lace, and silk gimp. This was a form of tape lace, with thick silk cords forming the tapes, held together with thin, neutral-coloured thread. It was used for both dress and furnishing, as was parchment lace, in which strips of silk-wrapped parchment were caught up in a silk net ground (plate 35). Gold and silver lace was widely fashionable, but very little survives because it was mostly melted down to retrieve the metal (plates 32 and 33).

The importance and expense of lace for furnishing and dress led to the production of many cheaper copies and imitations. Venetian needle lace was the most widely imitated technique (plate 34), and tape-lace copies were made of both Venetian and Milanese lace. Alongside the production of cheaper copies, extensive import controls and high tariffs in a number of European countries led to much illegal importation, and smuggling was an accepted part of the lace trade.

Outside the leading industries of Flanders, Italy and France, there were also smaller centres in other European countries, including Switzerland, Germany, Denmark and Spain (plates 36 and 37). In England lace making was well established by 1600, and the industry saw continual expansion during the first three quarters of the seventeenth century. Needle lace was made both domestically and professionally (plates 17, 39, 40, 41 and 42). In 1626 the bobbin-lace industry, centred in the Midland Counties (Bedfordshire, Buckinghamshire and Northamptonshire) and Devon, was said to maintain at least 20,000, and to supply lace for the export trade (plate 18). By the middle of the seventeenth century bobbin-lace making had in fact become established throughout Europe, partly professional work (in particular in charity institutions) and partly as a household skill.

❧ THE EARLY AND MID-EIGHTEENTH CENTURY

At the beginning of the eighteenth century lace industries across Europe experienced a severe slump, particularly those producing heavy needle laces. The grand and elaborate dress of the French court began to be simplified, the high headdress known as the *frelange* disappeared, and lace cravats, ruffles and flounces were to a large extent abandoned. Such fashionable accessories were now of plain muslin. The gradual revival was led by the Flemish industry, which perfected a bobbin lace with the softness and draping qualities of muslin combined with rich patterns based on contemporary woven silk design (plates 43 and 44). It left behind mesh grounds, and was now worked with patterned motifs closely juxtaposed, and open areas excluded. Its success was based on a combination of dense and complex design and exceptionally fine thread. It is at this stage that the diversification of Flemish bobbin lace into different technical characteristics can be seen. These were named after towns, such as Brussels, Valenciennes and Mechelin (or Mechlin when referring to the lace), although the lace was not necessarily made within these towns.

Two new technical characteristics were developed in Brussels lace in the early eighteenth century: the working of raised edges along some of the pattern parts, and the adoption of a distinctive delicate hexagonal mesh ground, known as *drochel* (although Brussels lace grounded with bars continued to be made). High quality needle lace was also made in Brussels, strongly influenced by the designs of *point de France*, but made with the fine thread developed for bobbin lace. It was much lighter in weight than its French counterpart, with extensive use of decorative fillings.

Fig. 4
601–1882
*Portrait of the Actress Peg
Woffington*, possibly by
Jean-Baptiste van Loo
English; about 1738
Oil on canvas
She is wearing a cap, fichu
and ruffles of Mechlin
bobbin lace.

12

The name Mechlin had been given to lace from at least as early as the mid-seventeenth century, and it may have been a general term for Flemish bobbin lace made with the straight-lace technique (as distinct from the part-lace technique, as used in Brussels). Much of it would in fact have been made at Mechlin, where there was a considerable industry. The particular thread used for it made it the softest and most delicate of all laces, and in the late seventeenth and early eighteenth century its muslin-like qualities were perfect for fashion; King George I of England wore a cravat made of 3½ yards (approximately 3.2 m.) of Mechlin at a cost of nearly £20 for his coronation in 1714. Mechlin lace was grounded both with bars and with a variety of meshes, and the pattern areas were outlined with a thicker thread of shiny linen (plate 51).

The town of Valenciennes was ceded to France in 1678 but retained its links with Flanders and its bobbin lace remained technically and stylistically a Flemish lace. The industry had suffered in the early eighteenth-century slump, but began to revive in the 1720s, its period of greatest prosperity being from about 1740 to 1780. Valenciennes was a straight lace (plate 47), using dense cloth work with fancy grounds and fillings, including snow flake, or *fond de neige*. Lace of this type is attributed to Binche, and it is likely that it was made in various towns across the France/Netherlands border (plate 48). Because of its exceptionally fine thread and the density of its designs, Valenciennes was very slow to make and consequently very expensive. It has been calculated

that it took up to 800 bobbins to make a strip of lace 10 centimetres (4 inches) wide, and a maker of the finest Valenciennes might produce only a single pair of sleeve ruffles in a year.

The Flemish lace industry spread across the Southern Netherlands, and included the Provinces of Brabant, Hainault and parts of Luxembourg. Antwerp, Brussels, Mechelin and Valenciennes dominated, but other towns also acted as centres for the industry, including Ghent, Bruges, Enghien, Mons and Ypres. Lille, like Valenciennes, had been ceded to France (in 1668), but continued to make lace of the Flemish type, and had a considerable industry in the eighteenth century.

The French needle-lace industry, centred in Alençon and Argentan, was badly affected by the early eighteenth-century slump in trade. It could not adopt the muslin-like quality that fashion required and that bobbin lace could assume; but with continued patronage from the Catholic Church and some court use, particularly in Spain, Russia and Poland, where French needle lace remained the prime lace for ceremonial occasions, the industry saw gradual development again. The difference between Argentan and Alençon lace seems not to have been one of technique, as thought in the past, but one of quality, with Argentan lace generally superior. Decorative meshes had an increasing importance in the 1720s and '30s, used mainly as filling stitches rather than primary grounds. In the middle of the eighteenth century crisper, heavier lace became popular again, and the use of horsehair to give a fine sharp edge to motifs was introduced (plate 52).

Bobbin lace had become well established as a craft in France, spread across almost the entire country. Its product was mainly lower-quality lace for home consumption, but there were some more important centres, making linen, silk and metal-thread lace, and also a significant amount of cheaper linen lace for export.

The influence on lace design of the patterns of fashionable silks continued throughout the first half of the eighteenth century, and resulted in further technical changes, including the return to mesh grounds in the 1740s when silk designs became more open. By this time needle and bobbin laces matched each other closely in their weight and texture. The design influences on high fashion lace included the styles popular across all the decorative arts, including chinoiserie and rococo (plate 54).

One type of lace unaffected by design trends, however, was blonde bobbin lace. This was a simple straight lace of undyed silk with small geometric patterns and open net ground, made in the Paris area. From the 1750s blonde lace had widespread popularity, a development that was part of the movement in fashionable dress away from heavy patterned silks to lighter fabrics. Its beauty lay in its open delicacy and the lustre of its thread (plate 55).

The English industry did not initiate any technical or design developments but concentrated mostly on the middle and lower end of the market. The third quarter of the eighteenth century was the most prosperous time, with enormous quantities of lace of all types worn, and legislation, in the form of import controls, in its favour. Honiton bobbin lace, in the Brussels part-lace technique, can be identified by its design (plate 56), but Midland Counties straight lace is likely to have been very similar to Flemish and is not readily distinguishable from it. The silk and metal-thread lace industry, established in London during the seventeenth century, continued throughout the eighteenth. This lace was used mainly for upholstery, ceremonial dress and uniforms and livery. The professional English needle-lace industry disappeared during the changes in fashion in the early eighteenth century, but it was carried on in amateur work, including a type of needle lace known as hollie stitch, a knotted buttonhole technique in which the pattern appeared in the form of openings between the stitches. This was used for insertions, in particular on baby clothes (plates 57 and 58).

The lace industry in Denmark was centred on Tønder, and the development of the industry paralleled that of England. The lace was similar in style and technique to English Midland Counties bobbin lace, using Mechlin patterns with a simple ground of twist net (plate 59).

In Italy the first half of the eighteenth century had seen the total collapse of high quality lace production, but a rise in the importance of cheaper lace of lesser quality. This side of the industry benefited from the rise in popularity of simpler thread laces in the 1750s and '60s. There was some small-scale continuation of needle-lace making in Venice, enough for the tradition to continue through to its nineteenth-century revival.

Among the other European countries where a lace-making industry had become established in the seventeenth century, Spain continued to be a large producer, and was also in itself and with its colonies a major market for the use of lace. Its industry expanded in particular during the third quarter of the century with the production of simple silk and thread laces. The mantilla (lace veil) and elaborate regional costumes sustained the Spanish industry during the later period when the use of lace in fashionable dress was much reduced. Significant production of thread lace and metal lace continued in Switzerland, and of metal lace in particular in Germany. There was in fact no European country in which bobbin lace of some sort was not made during the eighteenth century, since it was a craft thought suitable for the employment of the poor in charitable institutions everywhere, and it was adopted by folk communities on their ceremonial costumes and wedding linen.

Martha Cole & Martha Houghton
at the Sun in St Pauls-Church-Yard
LONDON.
Imports & Sells all sorts of Cambricks, Lawn, Macklin & English Lace, & Edgin; Where all Merchants, Dealers & Others may be Furnish'd, Wholesale or Retail at Reasonable Rates.

B. Cole sculp.

13

Fig. 5
E.2299–1987
Trade card for Martha Cole and Martha Houghton, haberdashers
English; about 1720
Ink on paper
Their wares included English and Mechlin lace.

Among the items of fashionable dress for which lace was used in the eighteenth century, lappets were a focus for the display of wealth and good taste (these were long streamers hanging down on either side of the face, attached to a cap-back and frill, the whole ensemble known as a lace head) (plates 47, 54 and 56). Their design and shape changed during the first half of the century, corresponding with fashionable textile design, and in particular the influence of the rococo style. It was Flemish lappets that matched silk designs most closely, because they were worn by the most fashionable women, and were seen in close proximity to high quality patterned silks. The chinoiserie elements of rococo were particularly favoured by lace designers, and from the 1740s to the late 1760s were of prime importance. In the second half of the century, as silk designs simplified, lace designs were similarly reduced in scale, and lappets became mainly composed of areas of expensive net sprinkled with tiny floral motifs.

For men the equivalent item of dress to the lappet for purposes of display was the cravat. The bib-fronted cravat was a feature of formal dress until the middle of the eighteenth century, and was also worn by women as part of riding dress. Designs for cravats were also influenced by woven silk designs, but their size allowed enough space for pictorial motifs, which often included chinoiserie. The other important costume accessory often made of lace was the sleeve ruffle, part of both male and female dress. Like lappets, ruffles changed in their shape and surface decoration during the course of the century (plate 44). From the mid-eighteenth century they were composed largely of muslin, net or gauze with a lace edging (plate 55).

Large-scale lace was still made for furnishings and for the Catholic Church. One important use was as decoration for the toilette table, in the form of deep flounces. Fine quality large needle-lace pieces were produced in particular at Argentan (plate 52).

By the 1770s the fashionable softer style of dress and the taste for simpler patterns favoured the use of gauze, muslin and net at the expense of patterned lace. *Drochel* net, plain or slightly patterned, made with bobbins, was an increasingly important element of lace, allowing well-defined motifs to be applied to a delicate background. Needle lace was generally more popular in this period than bobbin, incorporating small clear patterns on a delicate net, in keeping with styles of the day, and in Brussels a *drochel* ground was often used for this.

❧ THE LATER EIGHTEENTH AND EARLY NINETEENTH CENTURY

During the late eighteenth century there were further major upheavals in the fortunes of lace industries across Europe. Changes in fashionable dress brought in a more simple, often austere neo-classical style, and female dress, with neat bodices and long plain skirts, left little scope for lace, except in neck trimmings and shawls. The French Revolution of 1789 and its aftermath, affecting both the stability of centres of production and trade routes, and the availability of ready customers, accelerated the decline. The French needle-lace industry was particularly affected, since production at Argentan and Alençon collapsed.

Another increasingly important factor in the displacement of hand-made lace was the introduction of machinery designed to imitate it. In attempts to create machine-made net there were many inventions in the second half of the eighteenth century, mainly in

England, based on adaptations of the mechanized stocking-frame. These included point net, a delicate silk net that was first patented in 1778, but which was very unstable; a better version called double-pressed fast point net was patented in 1786. This was stretchy, made from single looped thread, and it had to be heavily sized before use and have patterns embroidered into it by hand; but it quickly became a leading fashion item. At the same time the French developed a machine net called tulle.

The most important development in following years was the invention by the Englishman John Heathcoat of the bobbin-net machine, the first version of which was patented in 1808. This produced a superior net identical to the twist-net grounds of the type of bobbin lace made at Lille in France and in Buckinghamshire. Each thread was wound on a separate bobbin, allowing for individual control and the eventual production of patterned machine lace. Initially, however, all machine nets were plain and had to be embroidered by hand. The bobbin-net machine had the advantage of producing net in considerable widths, while with hand-made lace the net had to be worked in narrow strips and invisibly joined. Among other significant aspects of the machine's introduction, it could work with cotton thread, and so spread the use of cotton into all types of lace making.

Most hand-made lace at the turn of the eighteenth to nineteenth centuries consisted of net, whether *drochel*, French needle-made, the twist net of Lille and Buckinghamshire, or silk blonde (plates 60, 61 and 62). The net ground was usually powdered with spots or tiny leaves, and the edges decorated with tiny patterns of linked leaves and floral sprays. On larger items more overtly neo-classical designs were used, including laurel wreaths and the Greek key pattern. All of these simple linear patterns had the disadvantage of being easily copied in machine-run net.

Gradually from about 1810 the neo-classical style lost prominence, patterns re-emerged, and tiny border sprigs grew into large curved sprays that in the 1820s and '30s filled scalloped edges (plate 63). This pattern worked particularly well with blonde lace because of the effect of the lustrous silk in the densely worked leaves and flowers, and the contrast with the extremely fine ground, now made with twist net (plate 64). Brussels, Lille, Mechlin and Buckinghamshire, all lightweight laces, also suited the style and were popular, along with embroidered machine net, but blonde was the overwhelmingly fashionable choice. During this period lace was gradually ceasing to play any part in male dress, but it increased in women's fashion, with growing fullness in skirts and sleeves allowing more scope for its use, and the popularity of veils and of overdresses made entirely from lace.

By the 1830s skirts had become even bigger, and in particular sleeves grew to enormous size, requiring

large lace collars and fichus for balance, and big hats with lace or net veils. For evening dress, women wore deep lace frills at low-cut necklines and lace flounces. Patterns in textiles were generally getting larger, and this trend, followed in lace, benefited hand-lace makers, since machines could not yet introduce pattern mechanically.

In the following decade the female silhouette was reducing in size, with sleeves smaller and skirts plainer in style. There was less scope for lace in day dress, but evening dress continued to be elaborate, with a change of emphasis from large accessories of muslin or lace to small but ornate pieces. As lace that was richer in both design and texture came back into fashion, designers and lace makers began looking to seventeenth- and eighteenth-century patterns for inspiration, and antique lace also started to be worn.

❧ THE MID-NINETEENTH CENTURY

A report on the Great Exhibition of 1851 estimated the number of lace makers in Europe at 535,000; those industries said to be commercially viable (that is, making lace for more than just local sale) were France, Belgium, Great Britain, Switzerland, Italy, Denmark, Germany, Spain and Portugal.

Of these countries the highest number of lace makers were in France. In the early nineteenth

century the best blonde lace had been made at Chantilly and Caen, mostly white or natural, with some black for the Spanish market. Another branch of the French industry was established at Bayeux in 1827. Heavy silk laces were developed there, and these were highly fashionable in the 1830s. As the fashion for blonde lace declined in the 1840s, the manufacturers of Chantilly, Caen and Bayeux introduced black lace worked with non-shiny silk, which was very fashionable up to the 1860s and retained its popularity to the end of the century. Until the 1850s the best was made at Chantilly, and the name continued to be used long after the centre of the industry had moved elsewhere. It was characterized by a delicate net ground and pattern areas, outlined with heavier silk thread (plate 71). As the market for larger costume items grew in the 1840s, Chantilly workers copied the Brussels technique and made the lace in strips to be joined invisibly, which speeded up production.

The French needle-lace industry had enjoyed some support from Napoleon at the beginning of the nineteenth century, including the imposition of regulations making it compulsory that the lace worn at court should be French or Brussels (plate 62). But the French lace industry in that period was really dependent on blonde bobbin lace and machine-made tulle. Needle lace returned to favour again with the growing fashion for richly decorated lace in the 1840s.

In Brussels trade had also been rather limited in the earlier nineteenth century with the dominance of blonde lace and embroidered nets; the industry also had to survive the climate of political instability in the region, leading up to the creation of the new Kingdom of Belgium in 1831. By the 1840s delicate but richly patterned Brussels lace had become fashionable again, and great efforts were made to improve and expand the industry in response to new demands. Lace schools opened and new designs were commissioned from Paris. By the mid-1840s Brussels was again the leading fashion lace. Hand-made *drochel* net continued to be used until the 1850s (plate 65), but machine net, onto which part-lace motifs would be applied, was increasingly used (plate 66). Bobbin-net machines had been set up in Brussels in 1834, using English cotton spun and gassed for smoothness. An increasing number of Continental manufacturers did the same. Except for the most prestigious pieces, most Brussels lace after 1850 was made with cotton thread.

Valenciennes reappeared as a fashionable lace about 1830, not made in Valenciennes itself but in other Belgian centres including Ypres. It was estimated that by 1851 the major part of the Belgian industry, more than 50,000 people, was involved in making Valenciennes-style lace. A more open form of the lace had developed in the 1840s, in which a dense white pattern stood out more clearly from a thin

Fig. 6
P.43–1942
Mrs Peter de Wint, by Alfred Edward Chalon
English; late 1820s
Watercolour on ivory
Her abundant lace accessories include blonde silk bobbin lace trimming her dress and at her throat, and a bonnet veil probably of black silk bobbin lace.

square ground. In Lille a simple twist-net ground had been introduced in the late eighteenth century (plate 60), and since this suited the light net-based lace fashionable in the following decades, Lille lace was popular, although it was never a high fashion lace, and its patterns could be copied in embroidered machine net. The industry declined towards the middle of the century because it was less suited to the boldly patterned styles coming into fashion. Mechlin lace was very important in the early nineteenth century as a trimming lace, but declined in the 1830s and '40s since it was not so suitable for the fashionable larger patterns. It was also an early target for imitation by machine, contributing further to the decline of its hand-made form, because it was a straight lace and could not take advantage of the technique of appliqué on machine net as the Brussels industry could. The 1840s saw the perfecting in machine lace of the technique of putting in outlining threads, and complex patterns controlled with the jacquard mechanism.

The English lace industry had benefited from the Napoleonic wars of the early nineteenth century. Trade barriers deprived the French industry of important English custom, and provided a boost for English lace makers. After these relatively good times the industry declined until the mid-1820s, but then the Midland Counties industry began to prosper again (plate 63). It was well organized, with good designers, and the 1830s and '40s were a high point for these centres. The Devon lace industry took longer to revive from the slump, suffering from lack of good design or organization. Queen Victoria chose to wear Honiton lace at her wedding in 1840, which was an important boost to the industry. Once it had royal patronage, organizers, businessmen and designers became involved, and alongside changes in fashion this brought improvements in design and technique to Devon lace by the mid-nineteenth century. In Ireland, the famine caused by the recurrent failure of the potato crop resulted in the establishment of cottage industries to give help to the distressed population, including the making of needle lace, in particular at the Youghal lace school in County Cork, which was established by nuns in 1852.

In the middle of the nineteenth century the market for all qualities of lace grew with the opening up of worldwide trade, the rise of the middle classes and a general increase in population. Hand-made lace was worn to demonstrate wealth and position; the top end of the market was stimulated, and in the 1850s and '60s a luxury lace trade had become established again, comparable in conspicuous expenditure to that of the eighteenth century. The industry was led by large international companies such as Auguste Lefébure at Bayeux and Verdé, Delisle et Cie of Paris and Brussels, who made lace for such leaders of

fashion as Empress Eugénie of France. Both of these manufacturers commissioned designs from Alcide Roussel, one of the outstanding lace designers of the nineteenth century (plate 67). They were prominent at International Exhibitions, exhibiting increasingly elaborate and technically accomplished pieces, but also made lower quality lace for the mass market. This was a period of experimentation, since manufacturers of hand-made lace recognized that technical and stylistic excellence was needed to compete successfully against the threat of machine lace. In Brussels, for example, needle lace was revived in a new form known as *point de gaze*, using mainly French designs of naturalistic floral patterns on a gauzy net ground. It became established as one of the quality laces, along with Alençon, Chantilly, Valenciennes and Brussels application (part lace applied to a net ground). The mass market for fashion lace was served by other centres such as Le Puy in France, making heavier, mainly bobbin lace, including torchon. Torchon lace was originally a form of peasant lace with simple geometric patterns and a mesh ground. It probably developed domestically in France, but spread widely across Europe in the second half of the nineteenth century.

Another technique widely copied in different European countries was that of Maltese lace. Lace making was introduced to the island of Malta as a philanthropic move in 1833. The style was based on the heavy peasant laces of north Italy, but the lace was made in silk, with the distinguishing features of predominantly geometric patterns and the extensive use of wheat-ears (plate 72). It was adopted as a fashion lace, being mostly black in colour (a little blonde Maltese lace was also made), rich in texture, and incorporating novelty while evoking historical style. The style was much copied throughout Europe, causing Maltese manufacturers to incorporate Maltese crosses into genuine Maltese work. It was taken up particularly in Le Puy, Barcelona, the Ligurian coast of Italy and the English Midland Counties, often worked in cotton rather than silk. English Bedfordshire Maltese in particular was of good quality and interesting design. There were also close machine copies of Maltese lace being made by the 1860s.

Fashions in lace from the mid-nineteenth century were still strongly affected by the popularity of black lace. This was reinforced by the patronage of Empress Eugénie, who had a love of lace, particularly black. As well as being a major part of the industry in northern France, black silk bobbin lace was an important industry in Spain, for both home use and export to Spanish America, and the machine-lace industry also grew up to meet the market. Much of the machine lace that survives from the nineteenth century is black in imitation of Chantilly bobbin lace, some of it of very high quality and design. Often in combination with black, the introduction of colour was a feature of both hand and machine laces in the 1850s and '60s (plates 73 and 76).

Black Chantilly-type lace was the most widely worn fashion lace in this period, but Alençon needle lace was the most prestigious. The newly introduced *point de gaze* increased in popularity alongside it, and was used for every type of accessory, being favoured for its prettiness and delicacy.

Net-based laces had an important place in the fashions of the time. The flounces that were needed to trim the enormous crinoline skirts of the 1850s and early 1860s would have been prohibitively expensive in hand-made lace, so inevitably most were of machine net decorated in some way. Brussels application lace was the most fashionable, in which the pattern parts were worked in needle lace, bobbin lace or a combination of the two (plate 66). In contrast was guipure lace (lace without a net ground), which had been reintroduced in the 1840s (plate 69). It was based on bobbin-made sprigs joined by short bars, and in Belgium it was made in a number of styles, under the general name Duchesse. In all of these laces, during the 1850s and '60s the depiction of flowers became more realistic, with new shading techniques introduced, typically decorating floral bouquets within bands of ribbon or architectural scrollwork (plate 65).

❧ THE LATER NINETEENTH CENTURY AND AFTER

In the years after 1870 fashion was more volatile than ever before, fluctuations critically affecting local centres producing particular styles of lace, and the lace industry in general experienced another downturn. Political events added to the instability of the market, with the fall of the Second Empire in France in 1870 and the end of Empress Eugénie's influence at the French court, and with the American civil war and subsequent upheaval in that crucial area for the European export trade. Changes in fashion were as ever the main cause of the downturn, with a move in daywear towards a clearer silhouette and a focus on drapery and trimmings made of the same fabric as the dress, although there was still potential in evening dress and in accessories like fans for displays of lace (plate 70). There was also still a demand for some lace trimmings and for furnishing lace, so the industry was reduced, but not to the point of collapse.

There were initiatives in some areas, however. This period saw a marked interest in peasant lace, with government backing for such industries to support local communities, and a growing middle-class interest in fancy work including peasant-style lace. The industry was important in the Erzgebirge region of Saxony and Bohemia. It received government promotion in the 1870s and '80s, making mostly torchon lace on the Saxon side, and tape lace on the Bohemian (plate 78). In the same period there was great enthusiasm in western Europe for Russian peasant embroidery and lace (plates 79 and 80). Torchon lace from the Greek Islands was popular, as well as bibila, a type of needle lace, normally made in the form of tiny flowers (plate 77). Such lace was shown at the International Exhibitions held in London, Paris and elsewhere, and introduced to wide audiences.

As well as encouraging peasant lace industries, official support, in the form of government backing and aristocratic patronage, was given to schools and other centres making reproductions of historical lace by hand. A major feature of the lace trade in the second half of the nineteenth century was the importance given to antique lace. The contemporary lace industry referred back continually in both technique and design to laces of previous centuries. Antique lace was cut up, re-formed and augmented with modern additions, since there was not enough genuine old lace to meet the demand at affordable prices. This encouraged the production of replicas. The Burano Lace School, on an island in the Venetian lagoon, was set up as a philanthropic foundation with royal patronage after the severe winter of 1872. It made lace of every sort, and from an early point was given high quality historical pieces to copy faithfully (plates 82 and 83). By the end of the century the School was making lace in purely nineteenth-century styles, and continued to produce pieces of this type and quality well into the twentieth century (plate 85).

Elsewhere in Italy, at Pellestrina a bobbin-lace industry was established in 1874, and made every type of bobbin lace in a mixture of antique and modern styles, including polychrome (plate 84). The lace industry in Cantu was known for its innovatory designs and high technical standards in bobbin lace into the early twentieth century. In Bologna the Aemilia Ars Society was making both needle and bobbin lace in historical and contemporary styles. A later development was the Industrie Femminili Italiane, founded in 1903 to organize local centres of lace making in all techniques on a national basis.

In Austria in the late 1870s the Vienna Lace School was established to promote Bohemian lace industries in a period of agricultural decline. It made the full range of laces, especially fine needle lace (plate 87). Irish lace was also revitalized during this period. Design classes were organized in lace-making centres, prizes awarded and commissions taken for important patrons, including Queen Victoria. The main centres were all based around convents, at Youghal, Kenmare, New Ross and Innishmacsaint.

Youghal had its own distinctive flat style and made needle lace in eighteenth-century patterns; the others made mainly raised needle lace in seventeenth-century Venetian style (plates 88, 89 and 91).

The English industry in the late nineteenth century was also reliant for its survival on patronage, and some improvements were made in design, quality and distribution through such organizations as the Midlands Lace Association set up in 1891. Among local movements a workshop was set up in the 1890s in the Lake District, making Ruskin lace, a type of cutwork in historical style, and the technique is still taught there (plate 100). Elsewhere the British were among other European settlers and colonizers responsible for introducing lace making to countries across the world where the techniques were previously unknown; for example, Midland Counties-style bobbin lace was taught in religious and charitable institutions in India (plate 90).

Another fashion swing brought quality lace back into fashion in the later 1880s, and it experienced a boom in the 1890s and 1900s, peaking between 1895 and 1905. There was a noticeable move towards uniformity, however, and a lack of initiative in design, perhaps for reasons of security in a temperamental market (plate 94). Lace of this period can be difficult to date and to attribute to particular centres of production. *Point de gaze* was the most fashionable, and fine pieces were made for exhibitions or special commissions (plate 92). There was also a revival in black Chantilly-style lace (plate 93). Brussels application lace was the most significant wedding lace of the period. The most interesting innovations were in central and eastern Europe, with fine lace made in Austria, Germany, Czechoslovakia and Hungary in art nouveau and modern styles (plate 97).

This partial revival in the fashion for lace and localized successes in the industry ended shortly before the First World War, the social and economic changes that were already underway accelerating the collapse of the hand-lace industry. Some efforts were made to keep it alive after the war, but the cost of hand-made lace combined with lack of scope for its use in the new fashions prevented its continuation as a commercial proposition. Instead, lace making survived in the later twentieth century largely through development of the techniques by artist makers, and as a thriving craft practised for pleasure by amateurs.

LIST OF PLATES

PLATE 1
5958–1859
Box for corporal (detail)
Silk and linen with bobbin-lace insertion in silver-gilt
thread
Italian; about 1560–70
The corporal is the linen cloth used during the
celebration of Christian mass.
Box 22 x 22 x 5 cm (8.7 x 8.7 x 1.9 in.);
lace insertion 17.5 x 4 cm (6.9 x 1.6 in.)

PLATE 2
T.297–1975
Border from a cover
Linen with cutwork and bobbin lace
Italian; second half of the 16th century
93 x 25 cm (36.6 x 9.8 in.); depth of border 14 cm
(5.5 in.)

PLATE 3
7523–1861
Baby's coif (detail)
Cutwork; linen
Flemish; second half of the 16th century
Centre panel 2.2 x 4 cm (0.86 x 1.6 in.);
length of strings 67 cm (26.4 in.)

PLATE 4
T.116–1959
Cover (detail)
Needle lace and cutwork; linen
Italian; 1580–1600
180 x 160 cm (70.9 x 63 in.)

PLATE 5
484–1903
Handkerchief
Cutwork; linen
Probably Flemish; early 17th century
55 x 53.5 cm (21.7 x 21 in.)

PLATE 6
288–1906
Handkerchief
Linen with cutwork, needle lace and embroidery in
detached buttonhole and satin stitches
Italian; about 1600
45.5 x 45.5 cm (17.9 x 17.9 in.)

PLATE 7
T.318–1975
Border
Bobbin lace
Italian; late 16th or early 17th century
205 x 10.5 cm (80.7 x 4.13 in.)
Given by Mrs A.M. Wedgwood in memory of
Mrs A.A. Gordon Clark

PLATE 8
T.148–1992
Border
Cutwork and needle lace
Italian; early 17th century
87.5 x 12.5 cm (34.4 x 4.9 in.); repeat 26.5 cm
(10.4 in.)
Given by Margaret Simeon

PLATE 9
T.153–1992
Border
Needle lace
Italian; early 17th century
153 x 16.5 cm (60.2 x 6.5 in.)
Given by Margaret Simeon

PLATE 10
T.154–1994
Border
Needle lace
Italian; 1620–40
227 x 26.5 cm (89.3 x 10.4 in.);
pattern repeat 38.5 cm (15.1 in.)

PLATE 11
T.33–1980
Border
Cutwork; cut from a panel of linen in imitation of
needle lace
Italian (probably Venice); 1620–40
388 x 27 cm (152.8 x 10.6 in.)

PLATE 12
270–1880
Cover
Bobbin lace
Italian; 1625–50
The eagles and the collar of the Order of the Golden
Fleece represented on this cover are the insignia of
the Habsburg kings of Spain. It was probably made in
Venice for Philip IV.
127 x 127 cm (50 x 50 in.)

PLATE 13
T.149–1992
Border
Bobbin lace
Italian or Flemish; 1620–30
195 x 14.5 cm (76.8 x 5.7 in.)
Given by Margaret Simeon

PLATE 14
T.342–1912
Border
Bobbin lace
Italian; 1620–30
71 x 21 cm (27.9 x 8.3 in.)

PLATE 15
T.150–1992
Border
Bobbin lace
Italian (Genoa); 1630–40
107 x 26 cm (42.1 x 10.2 in.)
Given by Margaret Simeon

PLATE 16
T.97–1973
Border
Bobbin-made tape lace
Italian (probably Genoa); 1620–40
396 x 12.5 cm (155.9 x 4.9 in.)
Given by Dame Harriette Chick

PLATE 17
T.320–1975
Border
Needle lace
English; 1620–40
162.5 x 8 cm (63.9 x 3.1 in.)
Given by Mrs A.M. Wedgwood in memory of
Mrs A.A. Gordon Clark

PLATE 18
1126–1903
Collar
Linen edged with bobbin lace, with tassels of knotted
linen thread
English (probably Honiton); 1630s
34 x 59.7 cm (13.4 x 23.5 in.)

PLATE 19
1135–1903
Collar
Needle lace
Flemish; mid-17th century
Maximum width 53.5 cm (21 in.),
maximum depth 21 cm (8.3 in.)

PLATE 20
T.99–1967
Collar
Linen, with bobbin lace
Flemish; 1650s
Lace 14 cm wide (5.5 in.)

PLATE 21
T.26–1949
Border
Bobbin lace
Flemish (Ghent); about 1665
The lace depicts Charles II of Spain, who became
king in 1664 at the age of four. The inscription
reads: CA SCCO REX HPA. As part of the design it is
reversed in some areas of the lace.
183 x 18.5 cm (72 x 7.3 in.); repeat 22 cm (8.7 in.)
Bequeathed by Lady Ludlow

PLATE 22
743–1870
Chasuble
Needle lace mounted on silk
Italian (Venice); 1660–90
This chasuble, together with its matching stole and
maniple, was bought by the Museum in 1870 for
£100, a considerable sum to spend at that time on
lace. One of the Museum's advisers recommended its
purchase: 'I do not think the Department is ever
likely to meet with a more eligible example of the
splendour with which such vestments were wrought
in the richest days of the Roman Catholic Church.'
106 x 69 cm (41.7 x 27.1 in.)

PLATE 23
T.20–1949
Collar (detail)
Linen with needle lace
Italian (Venice); 1660–80
Length of front panel 24 cm (9.4 in.);
width of each 17.5 cm (6.9 in.)
Bequeathed by Lady Ludlow

PLATE 24
T.18–1965
Handkerchief
Needle lace; linen
Italian (Venice); 1685–1700
37 x 37 cm (14.6 x 14.6 in.)
Given from the collection of Mary, Viscountess
Harcourt CBE

PLATE 25
770–1890
Border
Needle lace
Italian (Venice); 1685–1700
136 x 11.5 cm (53.5 x 4.5 in.)
Bequeathed by Harriet Bolckow

PLATE 26
T.158–1992
Cravat
Muslin with needle-lace ends
Italian (Venice); 1690s
Muslin 145 x 35 cm (57.1 x 13.8 in.);
each lace end 18.5 x 35.2 cm (7.3 x 13.9 in.)
Given by Margaret Simeon

PLATE 27
791–1890
Tallit (prayer shawl) ornament
Silk needle lace
Italian (Venice); 1670–1700
21 x 21 cm (8.3 x 8.3 in.)
Bequeathed by Harriet Bolckow

PLATE 28
T.870–1974
Panel
Bobbin lace
Italian (Milan); late 17th century
82 x 17 cm (32.3 x 6.7 in.)
Given by Christopher Lennox-Boyd

PLATE 29
T.259–1969
Panel
Bobbin lace
Flemish; later 17th century
127 x 11.5 cm (50 x 4.5 in.)
Given by Mrs O. E. Green

PLATE 30
T.354–1960
Flounce
Bobbin lace in linen and silver thread
North Italian; late 17th century
Circumference 389 cm (153.1 in.), depth 48 cm
(18.9 in.)

PLATE 31
T.134–1992
Furnishing flounce
Needle lace
French; 1685–95
This flounce was part of a set that was probably
divided up and dispersed in the 19th century.
Further pieces are known in a number of museum
collections. Its quality and elaborate symbolism
suggest that it may have been a royal commission.
340 x 64 cm (133.8 x 25.2 in.)
Given by Margaret Simeon

PLATE 32
T.124–1988
Christening blanket
Embroidered silk, edged with silver-gilt bobbin lace
Italian; 1620–50
This christening blanket belonged to the Muti
Papazzurri family (formerly Savorelli), and was used
at the christening of their first-born sons.
Silk 186.5 x 100 cm (73.4 x 39.4 in.); lace 11 cm
(4.3 in.) deep at ends, 5 cm (1.9 in.) deep at sides
Given by Jessica Teresa Cloudesley-Savorelli

PLATE 33
T.122–1977
Christening blanket
Silk satin decorated with gold and silver bobbin lace
Lace probably English; 1650–80
Silk 150 x 150 cm (59 x 59 in.), lace 14.5 cm
(5.7 in.) deep

PLATE 34
T.320–1912
Border
Needle lace
English; dated 1693
42 x 9 cm (16.5 x 3.5 in.)

PLATE 35
31–1898
Border
Bobbin lace, of silk gimp and silk-wrapped parchment
Italian; 1650–1700
54 x 18.5 cm (21.3 x 7.3 in.)

PLATE 36
57–1869
Altar frontal or cover
Needle lace (*frisado*), in silk and metal thread
Spanish (Valladolid); first half of the 17th century
226 x 74 cm (88.9 x 29 in.)

PLATE 37
T.337–1967
Flounce
Sol (needle) lace
Spanish; late 17th century
Border of late 18th-century bobbin lace attached
274 x 37.5 cm (107.8 x 14.8 in.)
Given by C. D. Pott

PLATE 38
T.229–1966
Furnishing border
Cutwork
Greek Islands; 17th century
Lower border of later North Italian-style bobbin lace.
Black glass beads were originally attached for eyes.
422 x 24 cm (166.1 x 9.4 in.);
pattern repeat 90 cm (35.4 in.)
Given by Mrs Walter Briscoe

PLATE 39
T.17–1909
Panel
Needle lace, with details in metal thread
English; 1600–50
The inscription reads: AL ADAMS GLORY AND PORE EVES
WAS DONE BETWIXT A RISING AND A SETING SUNE.
The lace is signed B E B.
24.1 x 23.5 cm (9.5 x 9.3 in.)
Given by Sydney Vacher

PLATE 40
T.150–1963
Band
Needle lace worked in human hair, with outlines
possibly in horsehair
English; 1640–80
16 x 4 cm (6.3 x 1.6 in.)

PLATE 41
T.198–1927
Purse
Needle lace, in silk and metal thread
English; about 1700
Height 10 cm (3.9 in.), circumference 30 cm (11.8 in.)
Given by Muriel Gardiner

PLATE 42
T.317–1912
Panel
Needle lace, with seed pearls and glass beads
Some of the raised areas have been worked over fine
copper wire.
English; 1640–70
The panel depicts the Old Testament story of the
Judgement of Solomon.
12.7 x 17.8 cm (5 x 7 in.)

PLATE 43
T.101–1970 (detail)
Apron, possibly adapted from a furnishing flounce
Bobbin lace
Flemish (Brussels); 1690–1700
102 x 126 cm (40 x 49.6 in.)
Given by Lord and Lady Dunboyne

PLATE 44
T.2 –1966
Sleeve ruffle
Bobbin lace
Flemish (Brussels); about 1700
Maximum width 16.5 cm (6.5 in.),
circumference 96 cm (37.8 in.)
Given by Miss M. Vigers

PLATE 45
T.99–1922
Furnishing flounce
Needle lace
French; early 18th century
410 x 63 cm (161.4 x 24.8 in.)
Given by Kathleen E. Cooper

PLATE 46
796–1890
Cravat end
Needle lace
French; about 1700
Two ends joined; each 41 x 32.5 cm (16.1 x 12.8 in.)
Bequeathed by Harriet Bolckow

PLATE 47
T.335–1913
Lappet
Bobbin lace
French (Valenciennes); 1720s
63.5 x 10 cm (25 x 3.9 in.)
Bequeathed by Mrs Tonge

PLATE 48
T.237–1926
Cap back
Bobbin lace
Southern Netherlands (Binche type); 1720–40
Height 24 cm (9.4 in.), maximum width 27 cm
(10.6 in.)
Given by Mrs Fred Egerton

PLATE 49
171–1887
Panel
Bobbin lace
Flemish (Brussels); 1730–50
90 x 43 cm (35.4 x 16.9 in.)

PLATE 50
T.44–1949
Apron
Bobbin lace
Flemish (Brussels); mid-18th century
96 x 108.5 cm (37.8 x 42.7 in.)
Bequeathed by Lady Ludlow

PLATE 51
T.50–1949
Cap crown
Bobbin lace
Flemish (Mechlin); mid-18th century
26 x 22 cm (10.2 x 8.7 in.)
Bequeathed by Lady Ludlow

PLATE 52
T.744–1974
Flounce (detail)
Needle lace
French; 1735–50
141 x 126.5 cm (55.5 x 49.8 in.);
width of repeat 72 cm (28.3 in.)
Given by Mrs E.J. Montgomery of Kinlochruel in
memory of her mother, Lady Noble of Ardkinglas

PLATE 53
T.22–1965
Flounce
Needle lace
French; mid-18th century
409 x 33 cm (161 x 13 in.)
Given from the collection of Mary, Viscountess
Harcourt CBE

PLATE 54
T.107&a–1916
Pair of lappets
Needle lace on bobbin-made ground
Flemish (Brussels); 1750s
Each 64 x 11 cm (25.2 x 4.3 in.)
Given by Margaret Jardine

PLATE 55
1043–1855
Sleeve ruffle
Silk and chenille bobbin lace
French; 1755–65
Circumference 96 cm (37.8 in.),
maximum depth 22 cm (8.7 in.)

PLATE 56
T.212&a–1989
Pair of lappets
Bobbin lace
English (Honiton); 1710–20
These lappets are decorated with lace portraits
probably representing John Churchill, 1st Duke of
Marlborough (1650–1722), and his wife, Sarah
(1660–1744). The Duke of Marlborough was Captain
General of British Forces and Supreme Commander
of Allied Forces. Sarah was Lady of the Bedchamber
to Queen Anne (r. 1702–14).
Each lappet 59.5 x 10 cm (23.4 x 3.9 in.)

PLATE 57
T.608–1974
Sampler
Linen embroidered with silk and linen in satin stitch
with cutwork and hollie point needle lace
English; dated 1739
Inscription: Mary Tredwel 1739
29 x 29 cm (11.4 x 11.4 in.)
Bequeathed by Mary Blanche Dick

PLATE 58
146–1907
Baby's cap (detail)
Linen with hollie point needle-lace insertion
English; dated 1776
Inscription: Thos Fry agedd 1 year 1776 Wroham
Kent
Diameter of lace 4 cm (1.6 in.)

PLATE 59
T.130a–1953
Border
Bobbin lace
Danish (Tønder); late 18th century
38 x 3.5 cm (15 x 1.4 in.)
Given by Susanne Salomonsen and Benedicte Helweg
through the National Museum, Copenhagen, and the
Tønder Lace Society

PLATE 60
536–1875
Veil (detail)
Bobbin lace
French (Lille); about 1800
89 x 82 cm (35 x 32.3 in.), pattern repeat 37.5 cm
(14.8 in.)

PLATE 61
T.252–1969
Veil or shawl
Bobbin lace
Flemish (Brussels); about 1800
153 x 158 cm (60.2 x 62.2 in.)

PLATE 62
3544–1852
Fichu
Needle lace
French; early 19th century
The fichu has been cut from a larger piece, and may
be related to the set of bed hangings made at
Alençon for the Empress Joséphine about 1809, now
in the Brooklyn Museum, New York.
72 x 48.5 x 48.5 cm (28.3 x 19 x 19 in.)

PLATE 63
T.245–1983
Stole
Bobbin lace
English (Buckinghamshire); 1820s
258 x 47 cm (101.6 x 18.5 in.)

PLATE 64
906–1875
Bonnet veil
Blonde silk bobbin lace
French; 1825–35
120 x 83.5 cm (47.2 x 32.9 in.)

PLATE 65
T.739–1974
Veil
Mixed needle and bobbin lace on a bobbin-made
ground
Belgian (Brussels); 1850s
185.5 x 175 cm (73 x 68.9 in.)
Given by Mrs R. Marchard and Mrs Aronson

PLATE 66
T.5–2003
Flounce
Mixed needle and bobbin lace applied to machine-
made net
Belgian (Brussels); 1860s
408 x 55 cm (160.6 x 21.7 in.)
Given from the Everts-Comnene-Logan Collection

PLATE 67
T.59–1949
Flounce
Needle lace
French (Bayeux); about 1867
Designed by Alcide Roussel and shown by Léfebure et
Fils at the Paris International Exhibition of 1867
260 x 48 cm (102.4 x 18.9 in.)
Bequeathed by Lady Ludlow

PLATE 68
785–1864
Handkerchief
Bobbin lace
English (Honiton); about 1860
Designed by Lady Trevelyan and made by
Miss S. Sanson
45 x 45 cm (17.7 x 17.7 in.)

PLATE 69
T.274–1982
Flounce
Bobbin lace
English (Branscombe); about 1862
Designed by Mary Tucker, a daughter of John Tucker, probably the leading Honiton lace manufacturer of the 19th century, whose workers made this lace.
The flounce was shown at the International Exhibition of 1862 in London by Messrs Howell & James, from where it was bought by a member of the British royal family. The *Art-Journal* wrote: 'Perhaps no British production has ever surpassed this work'.
500 x 100 cm (196.9 x 39.4 in.)

PLATE 70
319–1878
Fan leaf
Bobbin lace
English (Devon); about 1878
Made by Emma Radford
This fan leaf won a prize at the exhibition of the Fan Makers Company in 1878
50 x 13 cm (19.7 x 5.1 in.)

PLATE 71
T.63–1968
Shawl
Silk bobbin lace
French (Chantilly type); 1860s
Width 290 cm (114.2 in.), depth at centre 142.5 cm (56.1 in.)
Given by Mrs H.C.B. Lethbridge

PLATE 72
828–1868
Parasol cover
Silk bobbin lace
Maltese; 1860s
The inscription reads: GOD SAVE THE QUEEN.
Diameter 62 cm (24.4 in.)

PLATE 73
T.217–1982
Cap (detail)
Silk bobbin lace
French (possibly Caen); 1860s
length 121 x maximum width 29 cm
(47.6 x 11.4 in.)

PLATE 74
T.225–1984
Dress front
Bobbin lace
English (Bedfordshire, with a Buckinghamshire point border); about 1860–70
Possibly designed by Thomas Lester of Bedford
35 x 28.5 cm (13.8 x 11.2 in.)
Given by Elvira Strong

PLATE 75
191–1875
Furnishing trimming
Needle lace
French (Assimon, Delavigne et Cie, Paris); 1875
46.5 x 20 cm (18.3 x 7.9 in.)
Given by Assimon, Delavigne et Cie

PLATE 76
T.148–1911
Shawl
Silk bobbin lace applied to machine-made net
English (Devon); mid-19th century
This may be the 'chromatic silk berthe' exhibited by W. L. Gill of Colyton at the Great Exhibition of 1851
255 x 179 x 179 cm (100.4 x 70.5 x 70.5 in.)

PLATE 77
17 to b–1887
Collar and cuffs
Silk needle lace (bibila)
Cyprus; about 1886
Made by Helena Antoniades and exhibited at the Colonial and Indian Exhibition, London, in 1886.
Collar length approximately 66 cm (26 in.), cuff length approximately 29 cm (11.4 in.), width 7 cm (2.8 in.)
Given by D. Pierides

PLATE 78
871a–1884
Flounce
Bobbin lace
Bohemian (Erzgebirge region); 1884
39.5 x 49 cm (15.6 x 19.3 in.)

PLATE 79
1569–1873
Border
Bobbin lace
Russian (Orel district); about 1873
Shown at the Vienna Exhibition of 1873
79.5 x 13 cm (31.3 x 5.1 in.); repeat 13.5 cm (5.3 in.)
Given by the Agricultural Museum of St Petersburg

PLATE 80
497–1907
Towel end
Linen with bobbin lace in linen, silk and metal thread
Russian; 19th century
33 x 40 cm (13 x 15.7 in.)

PLATE 81
1997–1876
Border
Bobbin lace in silk and silver-gilt thread
Greek (Crete); 18th to 19th century
56 x 9 cm (22 x 3.5 in.)

PLATE 82
110–1884
Unfinished flounce
Needle lace
Italian (Burano Lace School); 1878–84
This piece is an exact copy of an 18th-century
flounce belonging to Queen Margherita of Italy.
It had formerly belonged to Clement XIII
(Pope 1758–69).
69.5 x 55 cm (27.4 x 21.6 in.)

PLATE 83
T.423–1971
Flounce
Needle lace
Italian (Burano Lace School); 1880s, in the style of
mid-18th-century *point d'Argentan*
355 x 30.5 cm (139.8 x 12 in.)

PLATE 84
T.249–1983
Dress front
Silk bobbin lace
Italian (Pellestrina); M. Jesurum & Cie,
late 19th century
38 x 16.5 cm (15 x 6.5 in.)

PLATE 85
T.29–1965
Stole or runner
Needle lace
Italian (Burano Lace School); about 1900
278 x 66 cm (109.4 x 26 in.)
Given from the collection of Mary Viscountess
Harcourt CBE

PLATE 86
T.225–1957
Bed curtain
Muslin trimmed with needle and bobbin tape lace
Italian; about 1875
Made for Queen Natalie of Serbia's wedding in 1875
Lace outside length 780 cm (307 in.), centre depth
92 cm (36.2 in.)
Given by Mrs Harold Exham

PLATE 87
T.422–1971
Collar
Needle lace
Austrian (Vienna); 1880
Designed by Josef Storck (1830–1902) under the
guidance of the K. K. Zentral-Spitzenkurs (Central
Lace Exchange), Vienna, for the lace
manufacturer J. Stamnitzer. The design was published
in *Blätter für Kunstgewerbe*, vol. 8 (1879), plate 49.
51 cm (20 in.), depth 16 cm (6.3 in.)

PLATE 88
T.18–1913
Border
Needle lace
Irish (Youghal); about 1886
Designed by Michael Hayes and made at the
Presentation Convent, Youghal, County Cork, Ireland.
Collected by Alan Cole while preparing his report on
the lace-making industry in Ireland.
30 x 22 cm (11.8 x 8.7 in.)

PLATE 89
Circ.531–1913
Border
Needle lace
Irish (Innishmacsaint); about 1886
Collected by Alan Cole while preparing his report on
the lace-making industry in Ireland.
49 x 11 cm (19.3 x 4.3 in.)

PLATE 90
6408
Border
Bobbin lace
Indian; 1850–70
Transferred from the Indian Museum in 1880
55.5 x 9.5 cm (21.9 x 3.7 in.); repeat 10 cm (3.9 in.)

PLATE 91
T.17–1913
Unfinished flounce
Needle lace
Irish (Kenmare); about 1886
Made under the direction of the Convent of the Poor
Clares, Kenmare, from a design by Miss Julyan,
Dublin School of Art.
Collected by Alan Cole while preparing his report on
the lace-making industry in Ireland.
45 x 44 cm (17.7 x 17.3 in.)

PLATE 92
T.366–1970
Veil
Needle lace (*point de gaze*)
Belgian (Brussels); about 1890
The veil was exhibited at the Chicago World's Exposition in 1893. It was bought there by Roxana Atwater Wentworth, who wore it at her wedding in 1894.
212 x 215 cm (83.5 x 84.6 in.)

PLATE 93
T.30–1965
Fan leaf
Silk bobbin lace
French; about 1899
Made by Georges Robert of Courseulles-sur-Mer, Normandy.
Part of Lady Harcourt's trousseau ordered from Worth of Paris for her wedding on 1 July 1899.
Maximum width 66 cm (26 in.), depth at centre 20 cm (7.9 in.)
Given from the collection of Mary, Viscountess Harcourt CBE

PLATE 94
T.46&a–1951
Pair of flounces
Bobbin lace with needle-lace fillings
Belgian (Bruges or Brussels); 1900–10
229 x 9 cm (90.1 x 3.5 in.); 340 x 14 cm (133.9 x 5.5 in.)
Given by Mrs A. Rodnanachi

PLATE 95
T.82–1946
Collar
Bobbin lace
English (Honiton); about 1910
Designed by Lewis F. Day
This collar may be the one exhibited at the Arts and Crafts Exhibition of 1910 made by members of the East Devon Cottage Lace Industry.
52 x 71 cm (20.5 x 28 in.)
Given by Ida M. Gabriel

PLATE 96
T.110–1936
Fan leaf
Bobbin lace
English (Honiton); 1910
Designed by Mrs Charles Harrison
Maximum width 50 cm (19.7 in.), depth at centre 15 cm (5.9 in.)
Given by the National Lace Association

PLATE 97
T.202–1921
Panel
Needle lace
Hungarian (Halas); early 20th century
Designed by Árpád Dékáni between 1902 and 1906
The figures represent the lovers Jancsi (Hansel) and Iluska from folklore.
13 x 13 cm (5.1 in.)
Given by Gyula Mihalik

PLATE 98
T.131–1986
Purse
Cotton and silk needle lace
English; 1986
Made by Ros Hills
13 x 5.5 cm (5.1 x 2.2 in.)

PLATE 99
T.85–B, H, J & K–1973
Samples
Needle lace
Austrian; 1920s
Designed and made by Eva Charlotte Roston (born 1893), who trained at the Vienna Lace School and became a professional lace maker. She worked first in Vienna then later in Berlin. These pieces are her order samples, made before she left Europe for South Africa in 1927.
B: each square 11 x 11 cm (4.3 x 4.3 in.); H: 227 x 6 cm (89.3 x 2.4 in.); J: 150 x 7 cm (59 x 2.8 in.); K: 52 x 6.5 cm (20.4 x 2.6 in.)
Given by Beata Lipman, Eva Roston's niece

PLATE 100
T.18–1979
Sampler
Linen with cutwork and needle lace
English (Cumbria, Ruskin Lace School); 1972–7
The sampler bears the embroidered inscription 'designed & worked by members of classes with Elizabeth Prickett / South Lakeland Cumbria / Ruskin Linen Work / 1972–77'. Sixty-two class members at the school were involved in making the sampler, over a period of five years.
93 x 65.5 cm (36.6 x 25.8 in.)
Given by Elizabeth Prickett

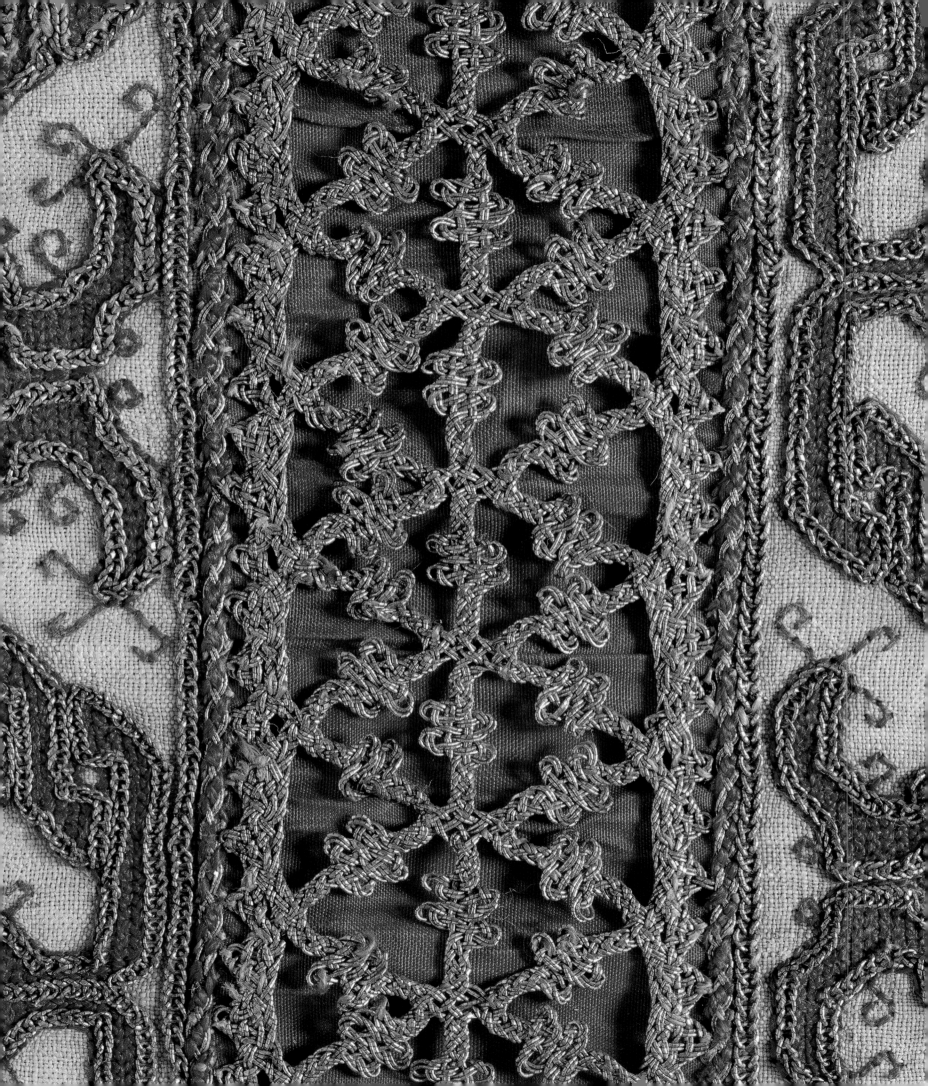

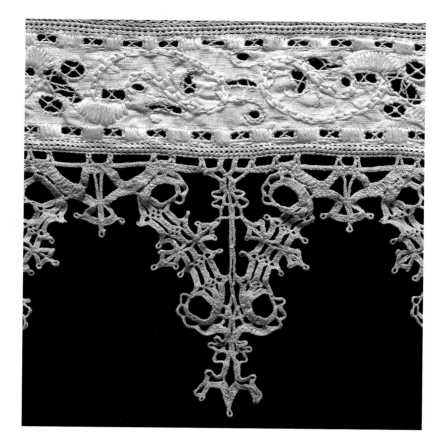

Plate 1
5958–1859
Detail of box with silver-gilt
bobbin-lace insertion
Italian; about 1560–70

Plate 2
T.297–1975
Border from a cover;
cutwork and bobbin lace
Italian; second half of the
16th century

29

Plate 3
7523–1861
Detail of baby's coif;
cutwork
Flemish; second half of the
16th century

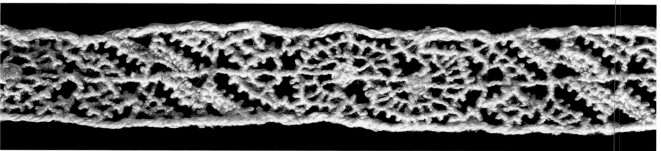

Plate 4
T.116–1959
Cover; needle lace and
cutwork
Italian; 1580–1600

32

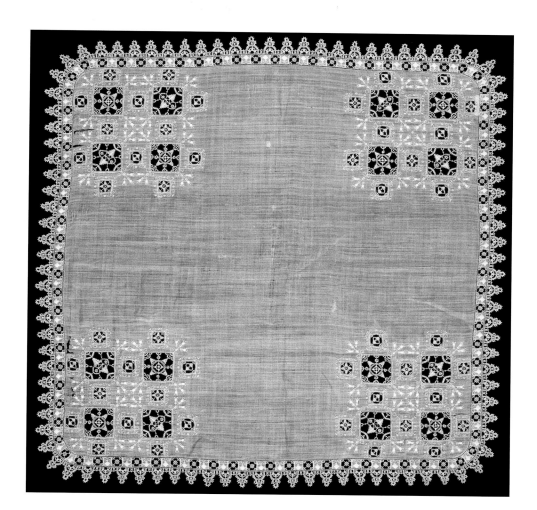

Plate 6
288–1906
Handkerchief; cutwork,
needle lace and embroidery
Italian; about 1600

opposite
Plate 8
T.148–1992
Border; cutwork and
needle lace
Italian; early 17th century

34

Plate 7
T.318–1975
Border; bobbin lace
Italian; late 16th or early
17th century

35

Plate 9
T.153–1992
Border; needle lace
Italian; early 17th century

36

Plate 10
T.154–1994
Border; needle lace
Italian; 1620–40

Plate 11
T.33–1980
Border; cutwork
Italian; 1620–40

37

Plate 12
270–1880
Cover; bobbin lace
Italian; 1625–50

Plate 12
details

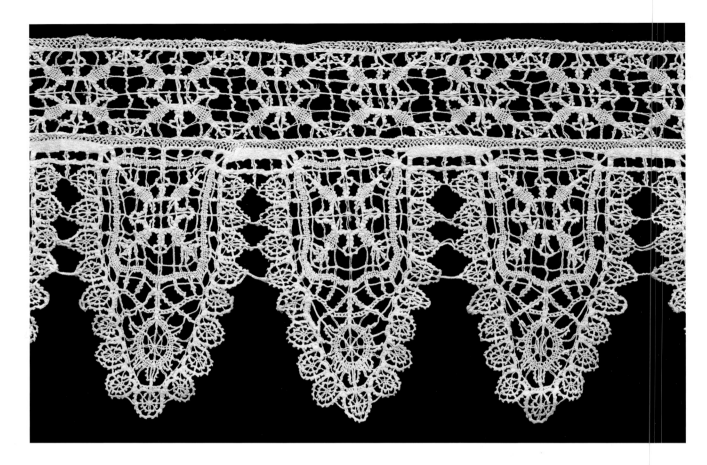

Plate 13
T.149–1992
Border; bobbin lace
Italian or Flemish; 1620–30

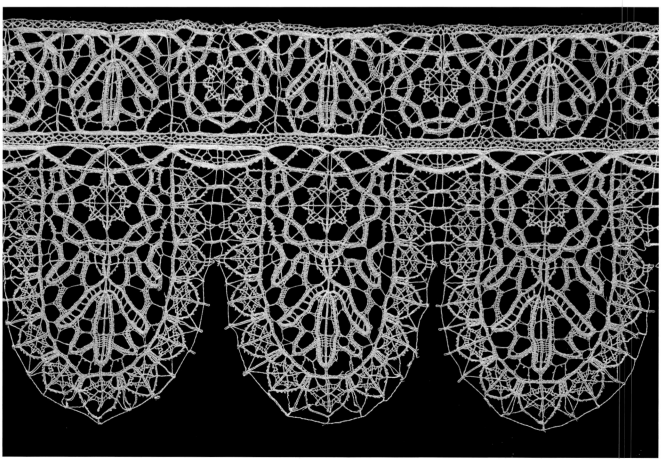

Plate 14
T.342–1912
Border; bobbin lace
Italian; 1620–30

Plate 15
T.150–1992
Border; bobbin lace
Italian (Genoa); 1630–40

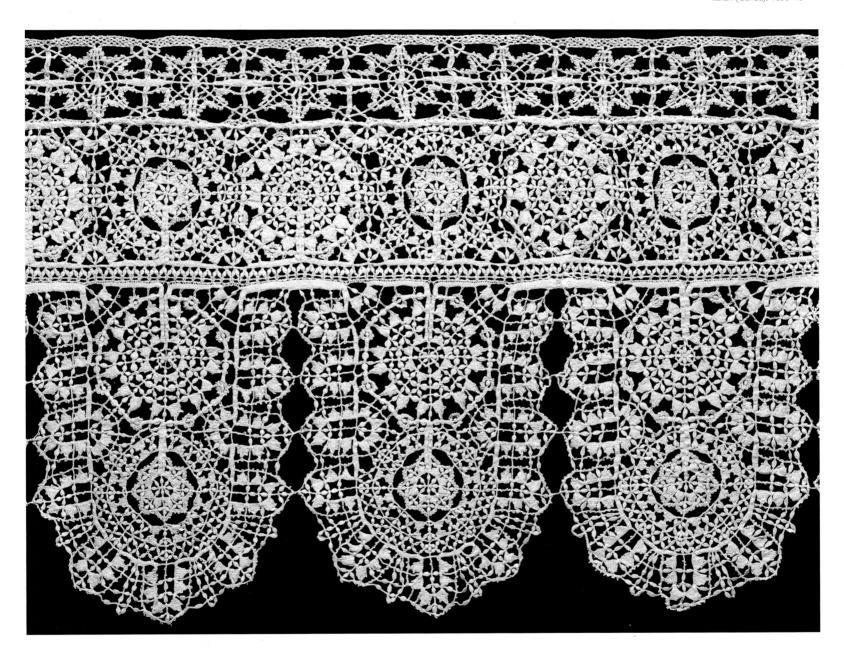

41

Plate 17
T.320–1975
Border; needle lace
English; 1620–40

Plate 16
T.97–1973
Border; bobbin-made
tape lace
Italian (probably Genoa);
1620–40

42

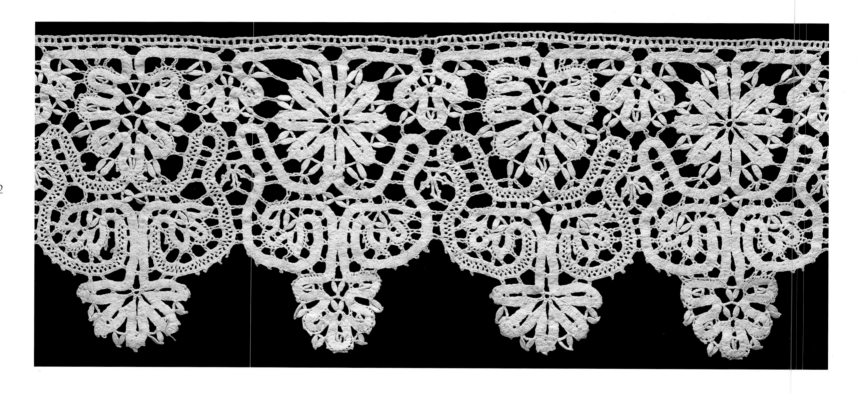

Plate 18
1126–1903
Collar; bobbin lace
English; 1630s

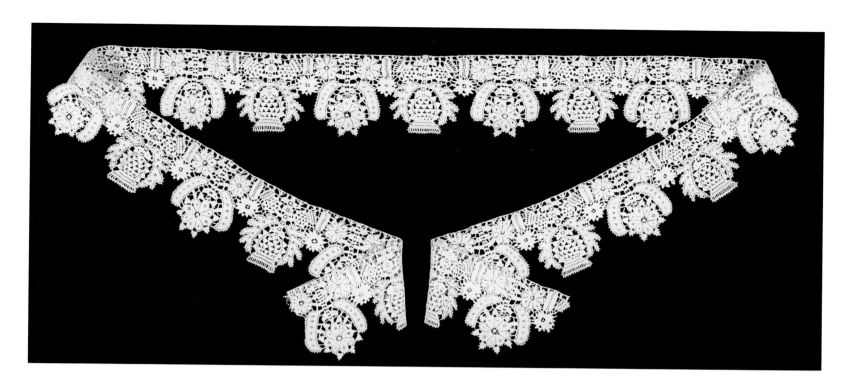

Plate 19
1135–1903
Collar; needle lace
Flemish; mid-17th century

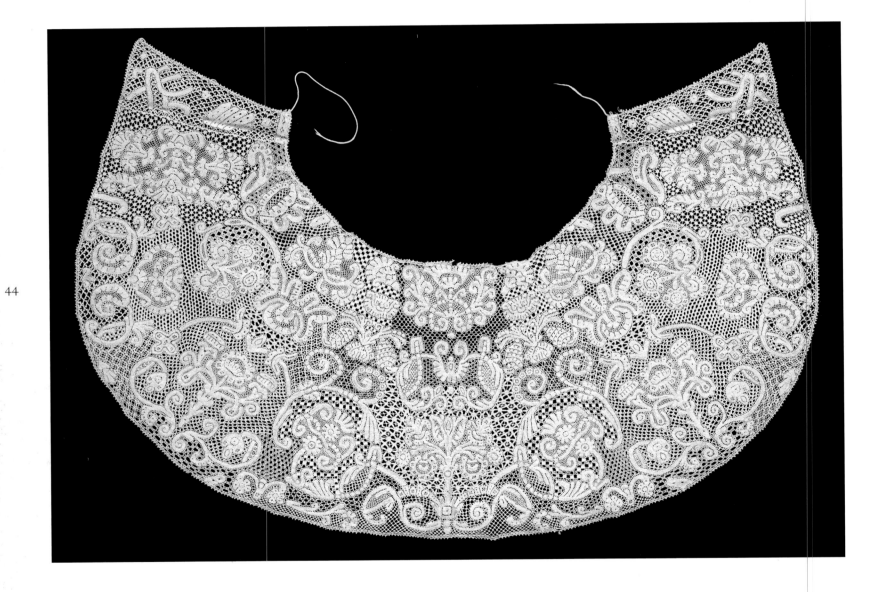

44

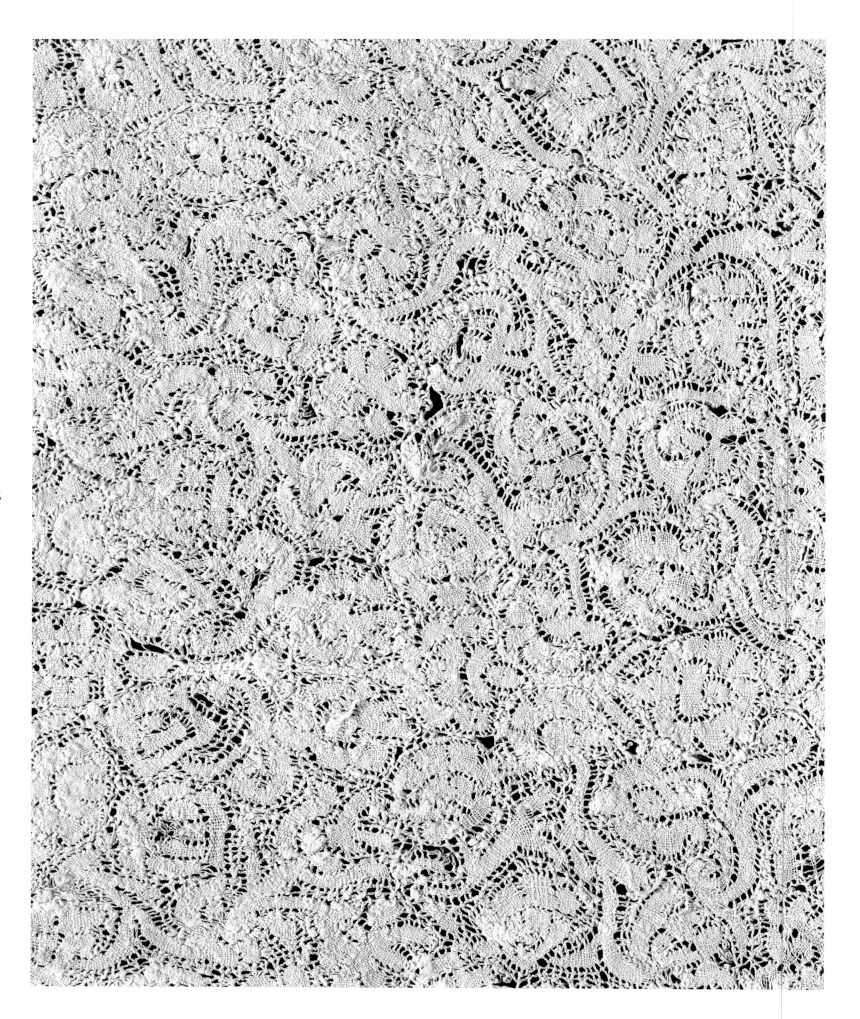

Plate 20
T.99–1967
Collar, with bobbin lace
Flemish; 1650s

47

Plate 21
T.26–1949
Border; bobbin lace
Flemish; about 1665

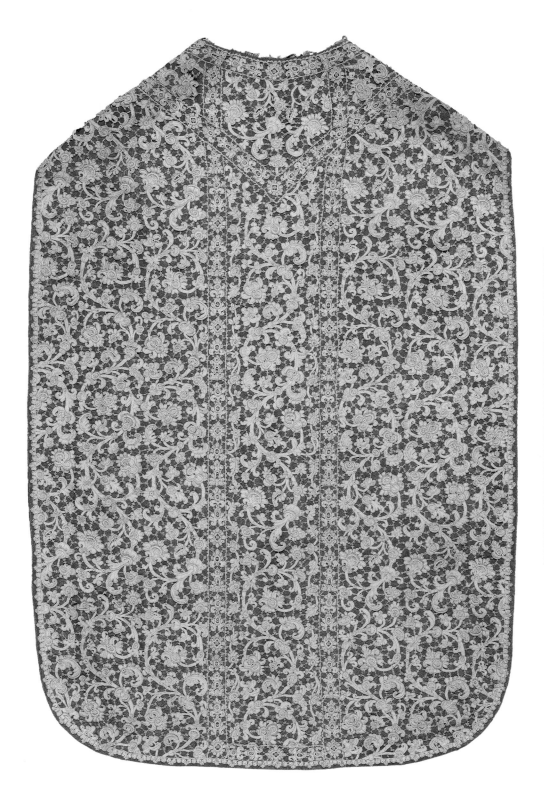

Plate 22
743–1870
Chasuble; needle lace
Italian; 1660–90

49

Plate 24
T.18–1965
Handkerchief; needle lace
Italian; 1685–1700

Plate 23
T.20–1949
Collar; needle lace
Italian; 1660–80

50

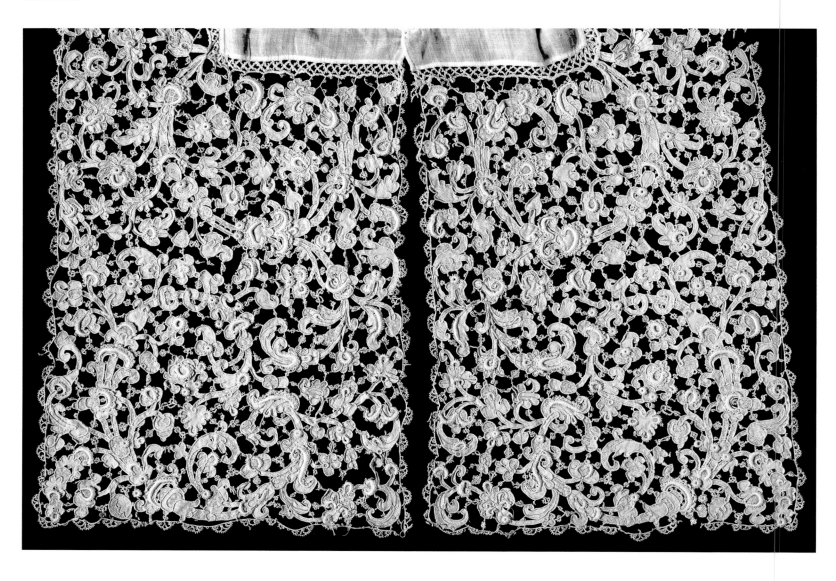

Plate 25
770–1890
Border; needle lace
Italian; 1685–1700

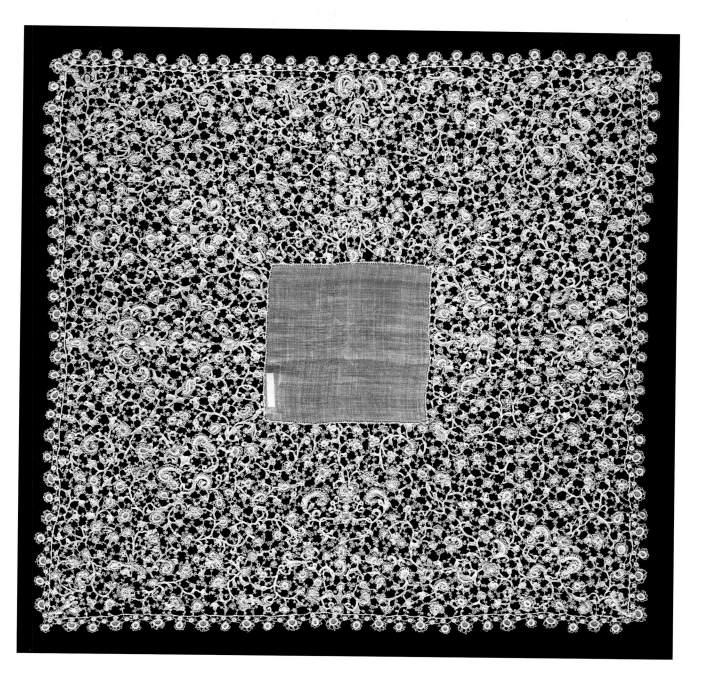

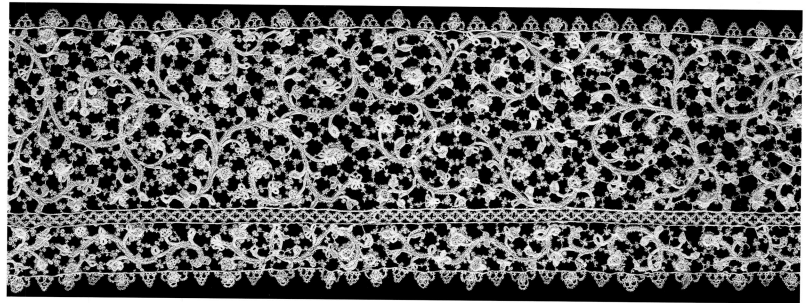

52

Plate 26
T.158–1992
Cravat; needle lace
Italian; 1690s

Plate 27
791–1890
Tallit (prayer shawl)
ornament; silk needle lace
Italian; 1670–1700

53

Plate 28
T.870–1974
Panel; bobbin lace
Italian; late 17th century

54

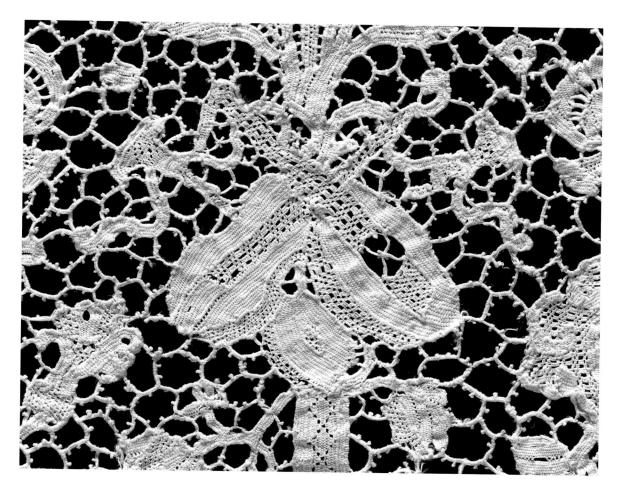

Plate 31
T.134–1992
details

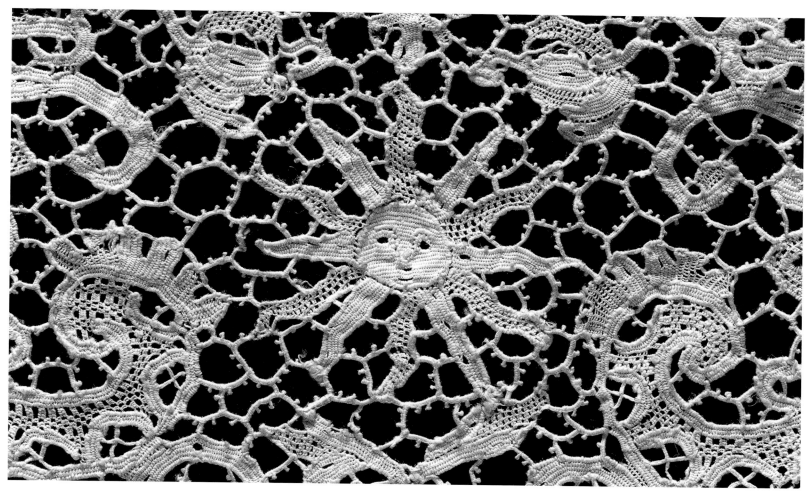

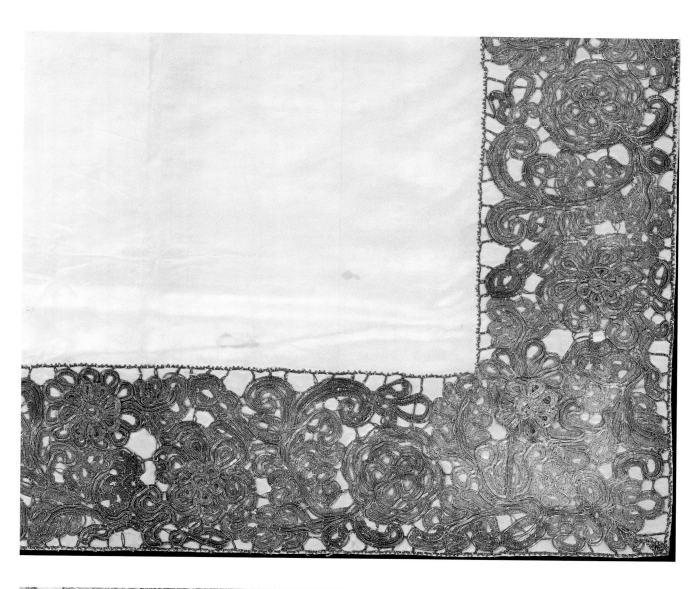

opposite
Plate 32
T.124–1988
Christening blanket edged
with silver-gilt bobbin lace
Italian; 1620–50

61

Plate 33
T.122–1977
Christening blanket
decorated with gold
and silver bobbin lace
Probably English; 1650–80

Plate 34
T.320–1912
Border; needle lace
English; dated 1693

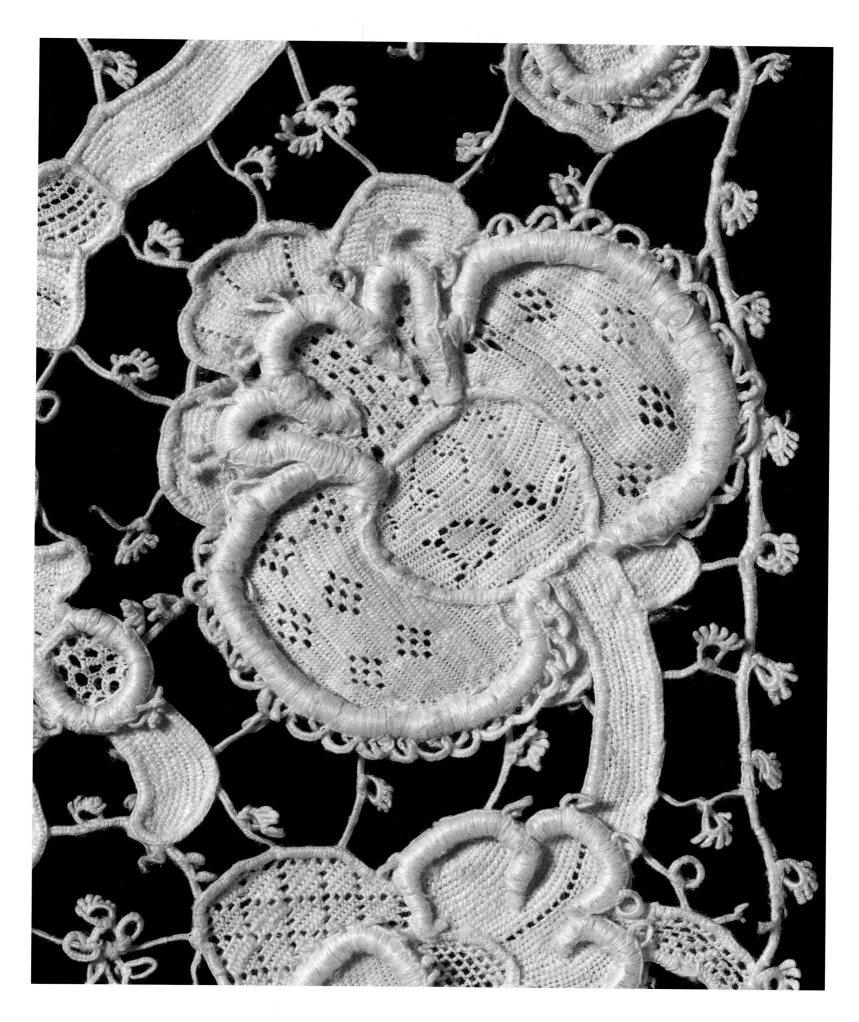

63

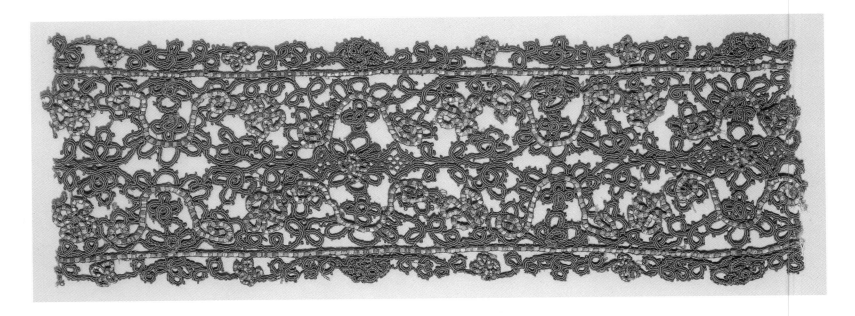

Plate 35
31–1898
Border; bobbin lace of silk
gimp and silk-wrapped
parchment
Italian; 1650–1700

64

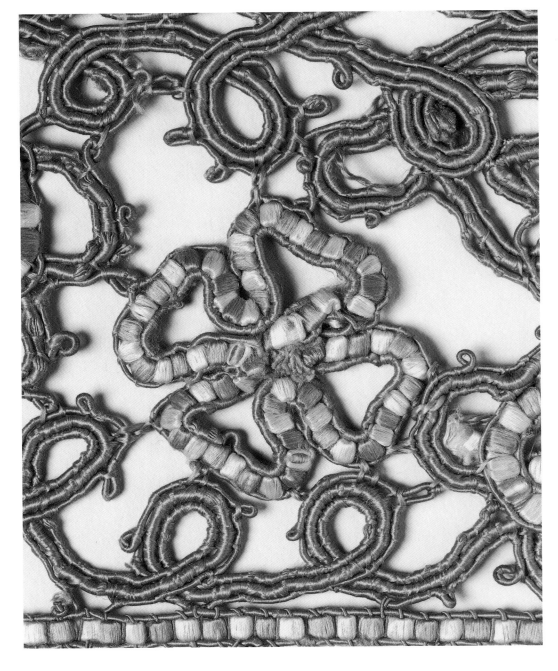

Plate 36
57–1869
Altar frontal or cover;
silk and metal-thread
needle lace
Spanish; first half of the
17th century

Plate 37
T.337–1967
Flounce; *sol* (needle) lace
Spanish; late 17th century

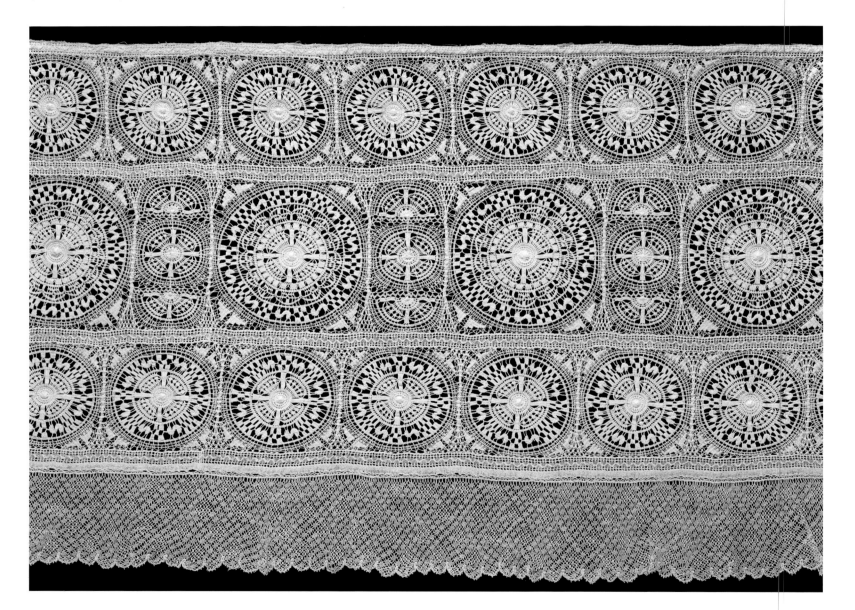

Plate 38
T.229–1966
Furnishing border; cutwork
Greek Islands; 17th century

67

Plate 39
T.17–1909
Panel; needle lace
English; 1600–50

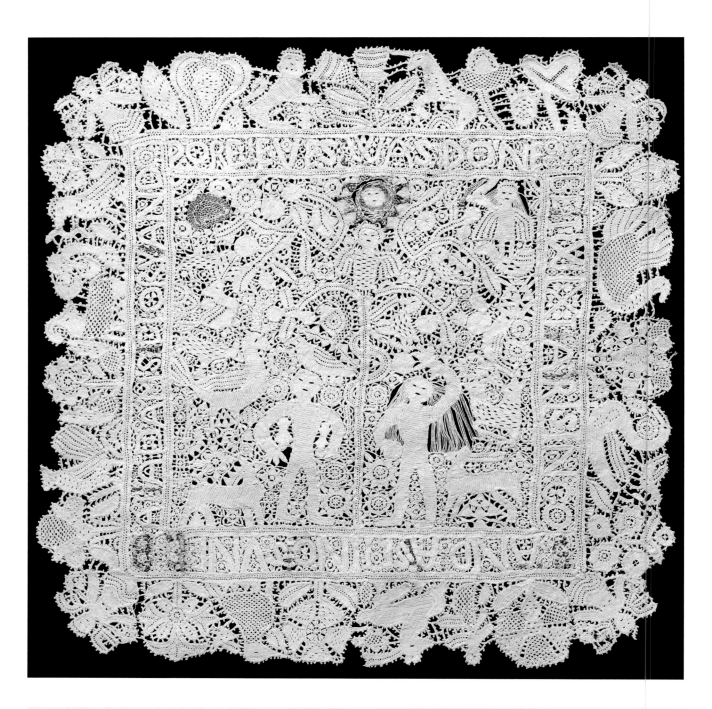

Plate 40
T.150–1963
Band; needle lace worked
in hair
English; 1640–80

Plate 41
T.198–1927
Purse; silk and metal-thread
needle lace
English; about 1700

Plate 42
T.317–1912
Panel; needle lace
English; 1640–70

opposite
Plate 43
T.101–1970
Detail of apron; bobbin lace
Flemish (Brussels);
1690–1700

73

opposite
Plate 44
T.2 –1966
Sleeve ruffle; bobbin lace
Flemish (Brussels);
about 1700

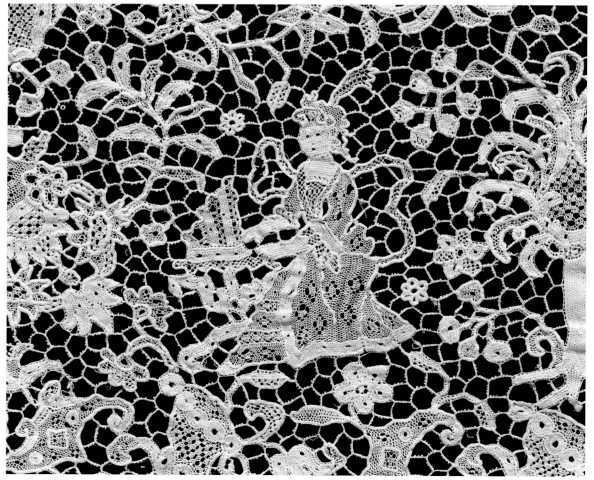

Plate 46
796–1890
Cravat end; needle lace
French; about 1700

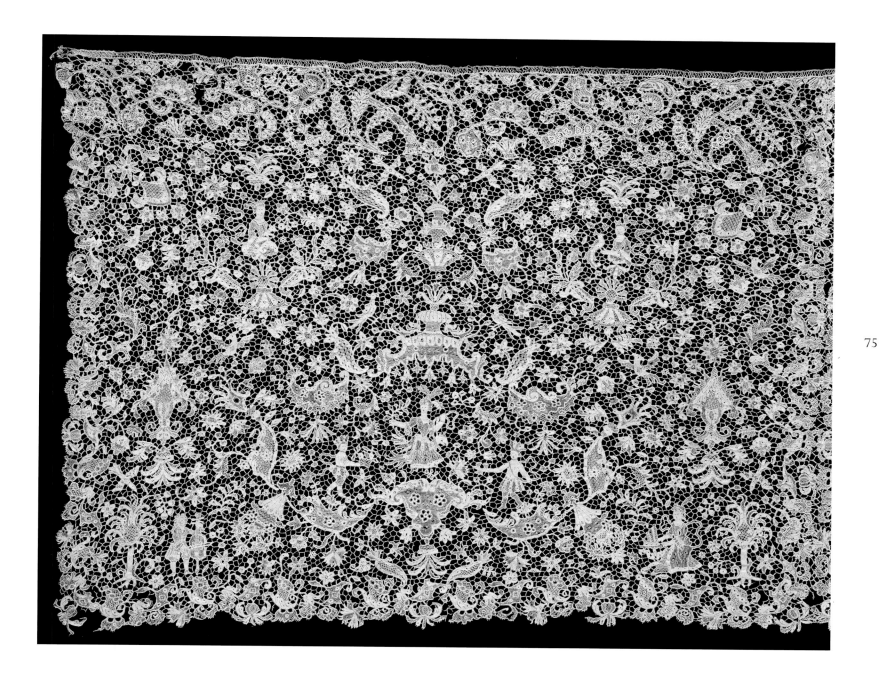

75

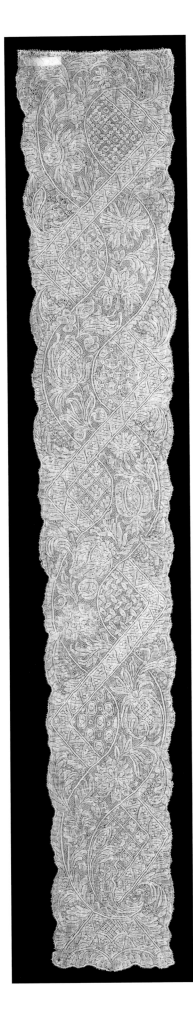

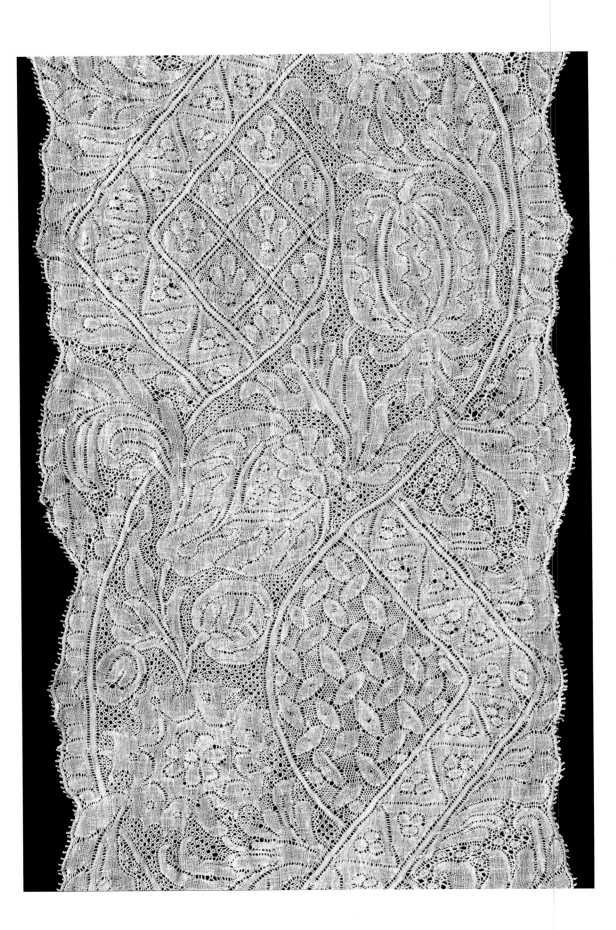

Plate 47
T.335–1913
Lappet; bobbin lace
French (Valenciennes);
1720s

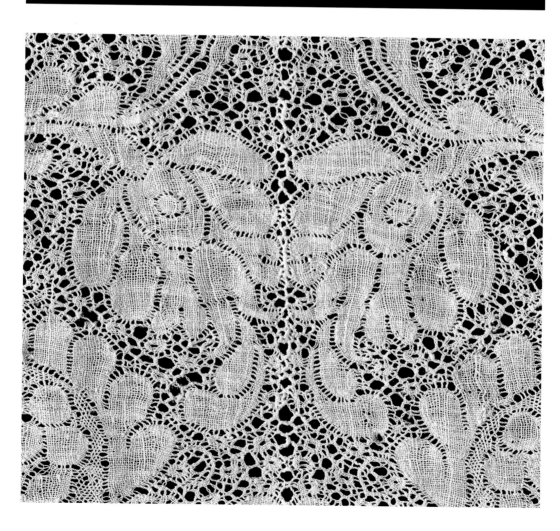

Plate 48
T.237–1926
Cap back; bobbin lace
Southern Netherlands;
1720–40

Plate 49
171–1887
Panel; bobbin lace
Flemish (Brussels); 1730–50

78

80

Plate 50
T.44—1949
Apron; bobbin lace
Flemish (Brussels); mid-18th century

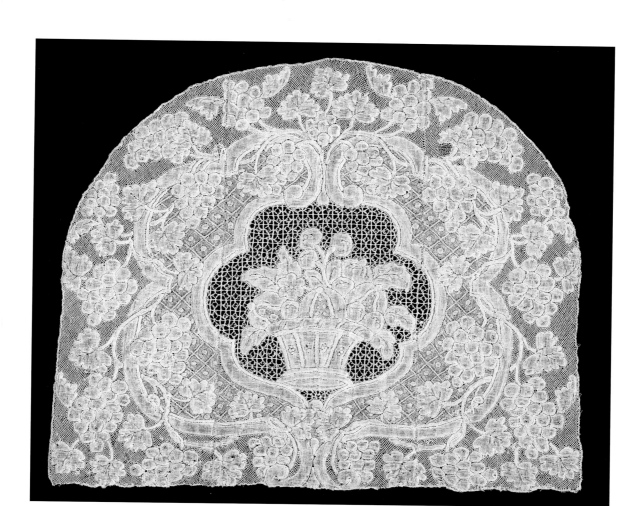

Plate 51
T.50–1949
Cap crown; bobbin lace
Flemish (Mechlin);
mid-18th century

Plate 52
T.744–1974
Flounce; needle lace
French; 1735–50

82

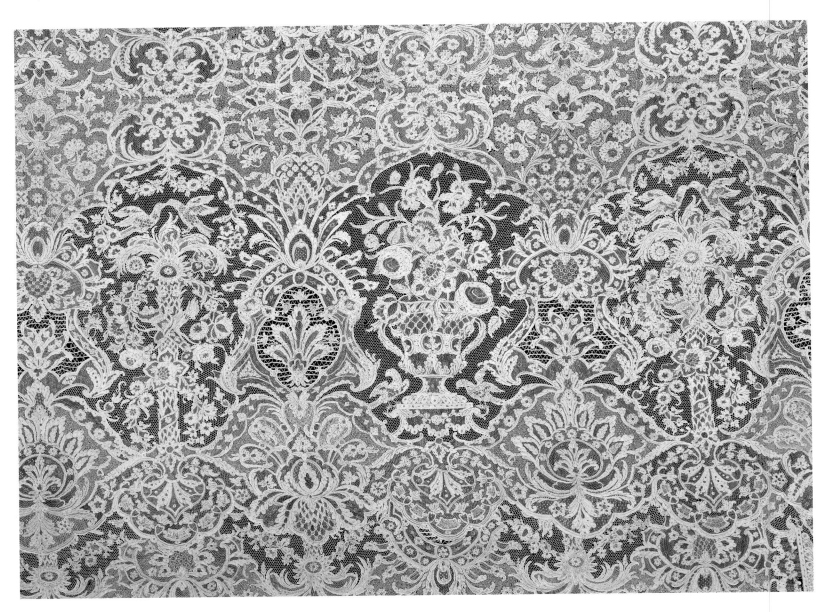

Plate 52
T.744–1974
detail

83

Plate 53
T.22–1965
Flounce; needle lace
French; mid-18th century

85

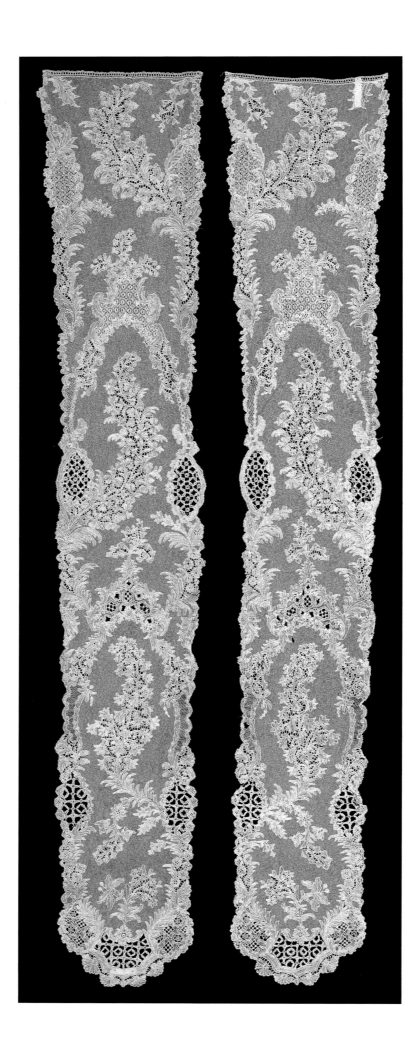

Plate 54
T.107&a–1916
Pair of lappets; needle lace
on bobbin-made ground
Flemish (Brussels); 1750s

Plate 55
1043–1855
Sleeve ruffle; silk and chenille
bobbin lace
French; 1755–65

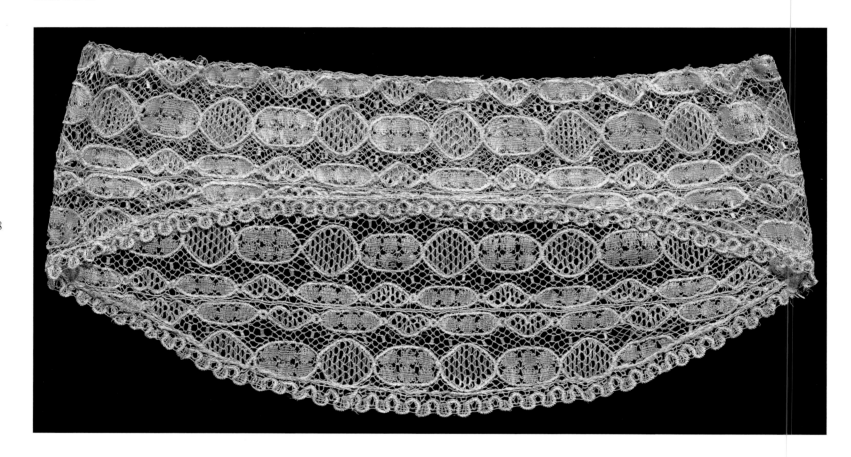

Plate 58
146–1907
Baby's cap; detail with hollie
point needle lace
English; dated 1776

Plate 59
T.130a–1953
Border; bobbin lace
Danish (Tønder);
late 18th century

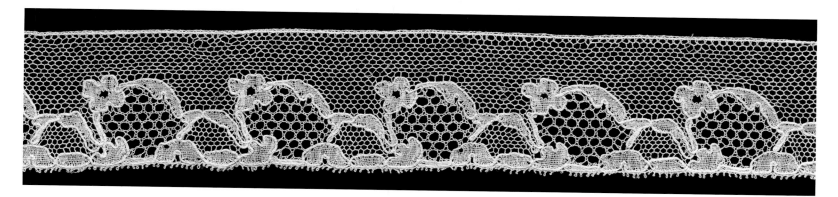

Plate 60
536–1875
Veil; bobbin lace
French (Lille); about 1800

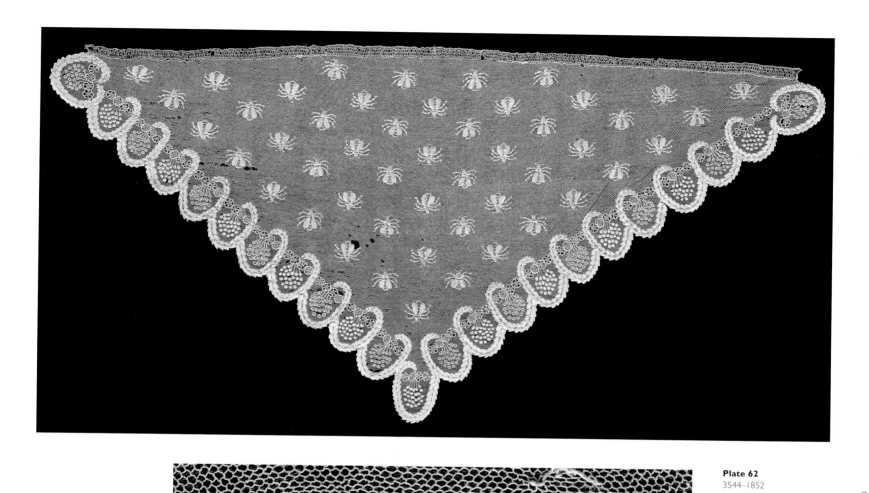

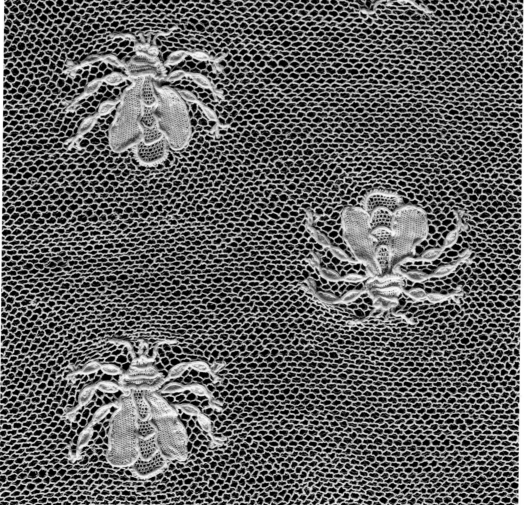

95

Plate 62
3544–1852
Fichu; needle lace
French; early 19th century

opposite
Plate 61
T.252–1969
Veil or shawl; bobbin lace
Flemish (Brussels);
About 1800

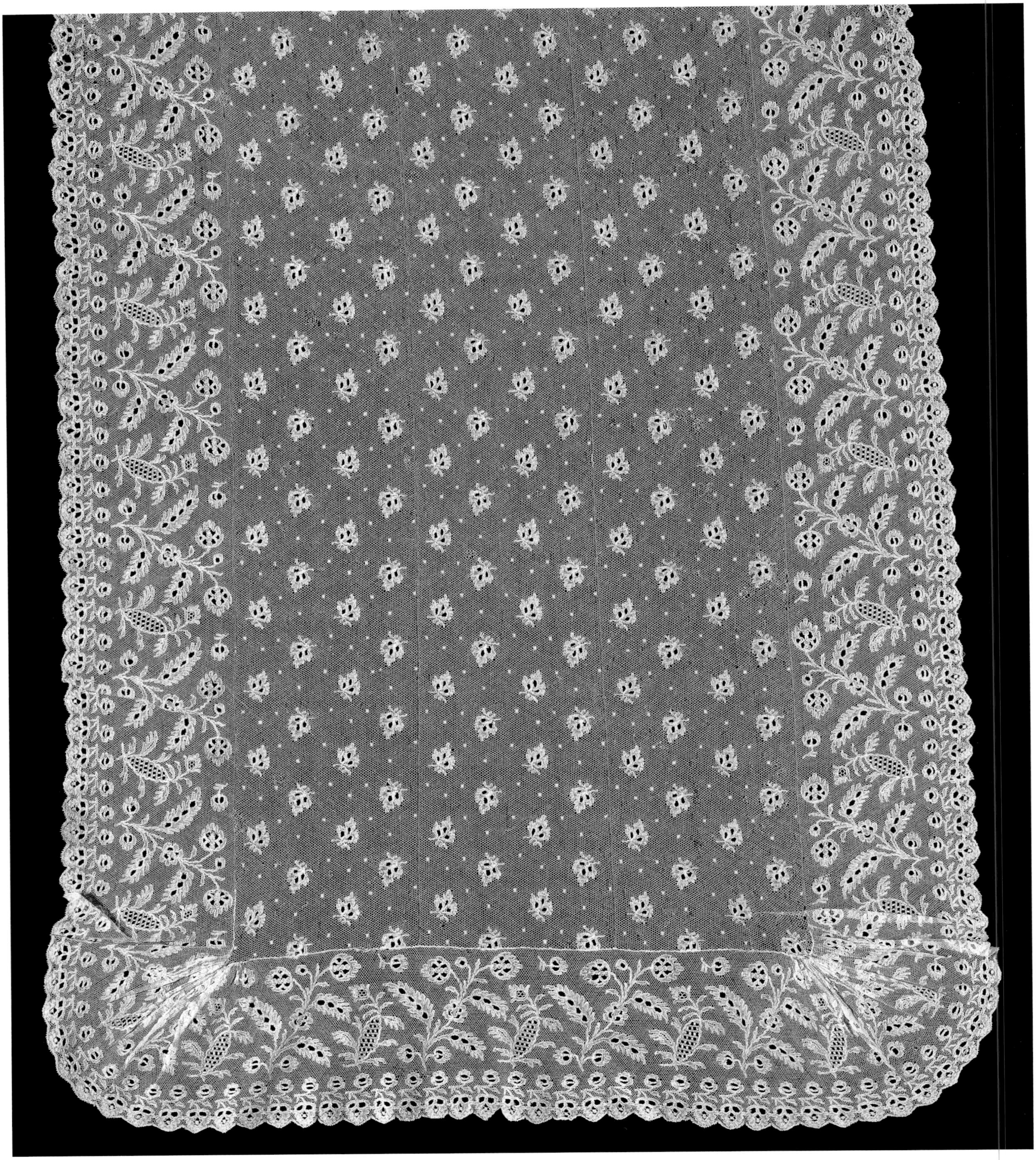

97

Plate 64
906–1875
Bonnet veil; silk bobbin lace
French; 1825–35

99

Plate 66
T.5–2003
Flounce; mixed needle and
bobbin lace
Belgian (Brussels); 1860s

100

107

Plate 69
T.274–1982
Flounce; bobbin lace
English (Branscombe);
about 1862

Plate 70
319–1878
Fan leaf; bobbin lace
English (Devon); about 1878

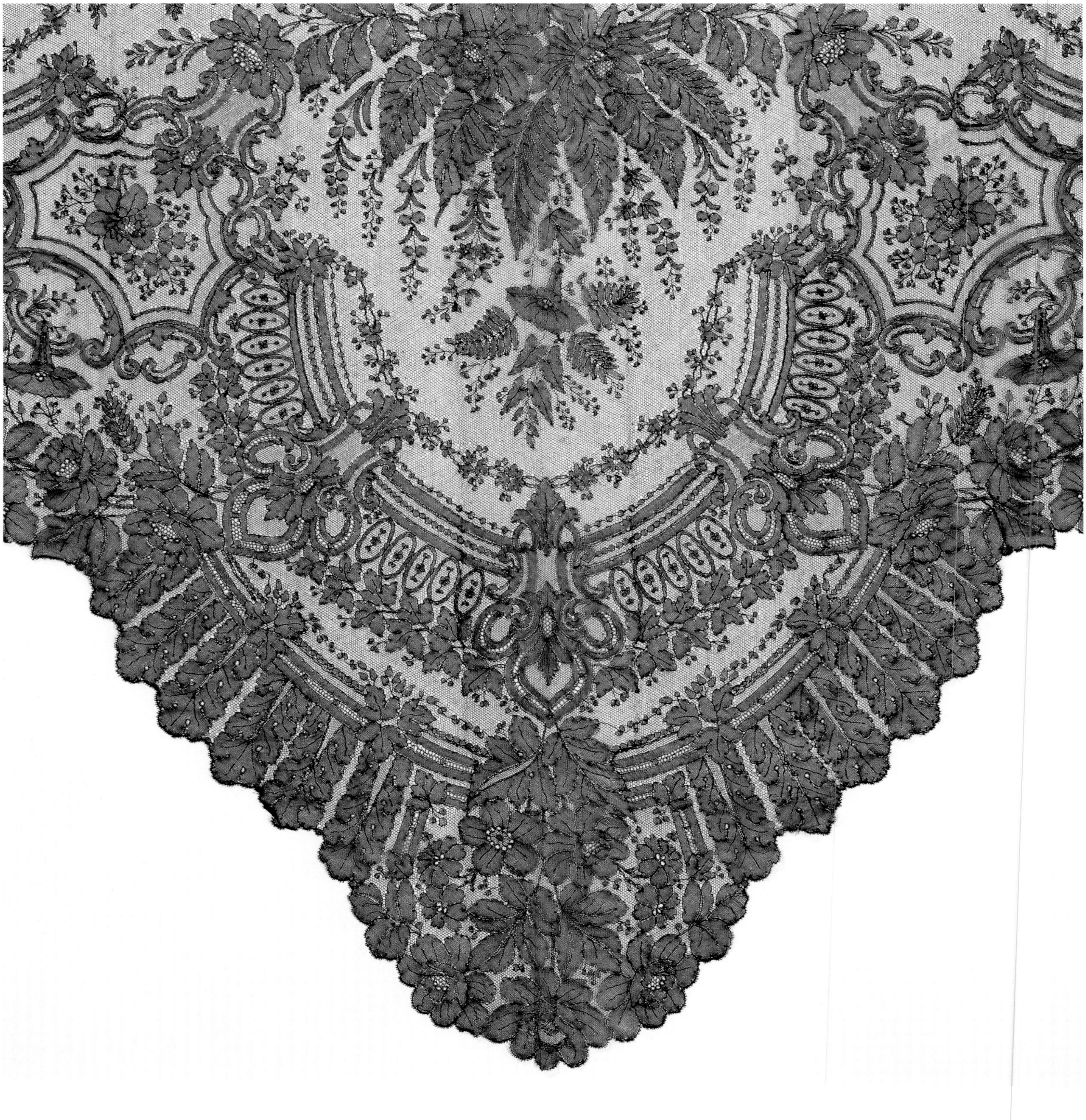

Plate 71
T.63–1968
Shawl; silk bobbin lace
French (Chantilly type);
1860s

Plate 72
828–1868
Parasol cover;
silk bobbin lace
Maltese; 1860s

112

113

opposite
Plate 74
T.225–1984
Dress front; bobbin lace
English (Bedfordshire);
about 1860–70

115

Plate 76
T.148–1911
Shawl; silk bobbin lace
English (Devon);
mid-19th century

116

Plate 77
17 to b–1887
Collar and cuffs;
silk needle lace
Cyprus; about 1886

118

opposite
Plate 79
1569–1873
Border; bobbin lace
Russian (Orel district);
about 1873

Plate 80
497–1907
Towel end; linen, silk and
metal-thread bobbin lace
Russian; 19th century

127

Plate 86
T.225–1957
Bed curtain; needle and
bobbin tape lace
Italian; about 1875

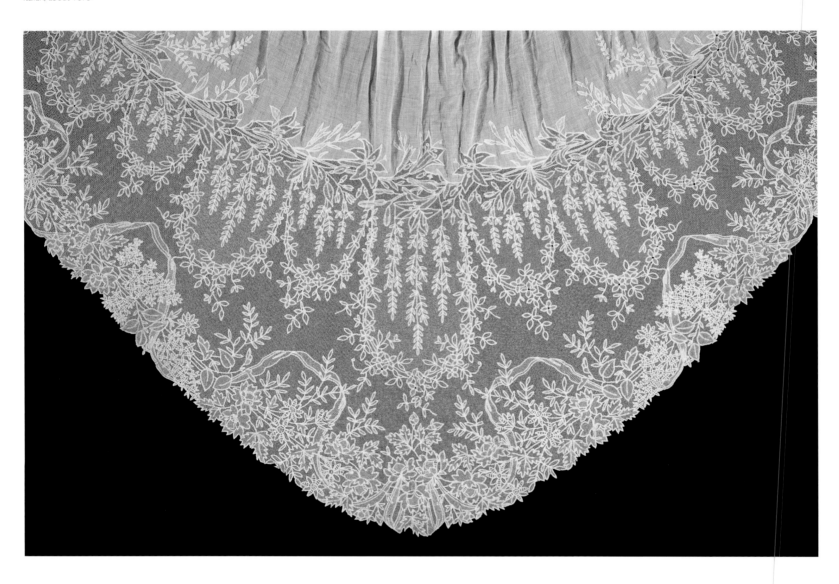

Plate 87
T.422–1971
Collar; needle lace
Austrian (Vienna); 1880

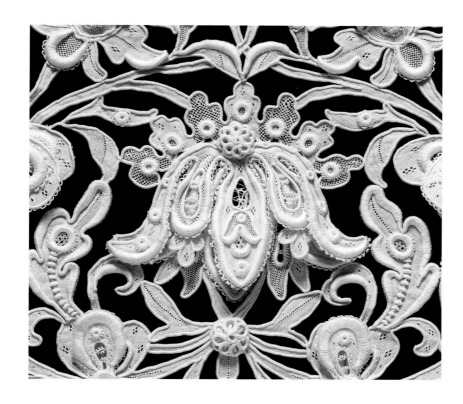

129

130

Plate 88
T.18–1913
Border; needle lace
Irish (Youghal); about 1886

131

Plate 89
Circ.531–1913
Border; needle lace
Irish (Innishmacsaint);
about 1886

132

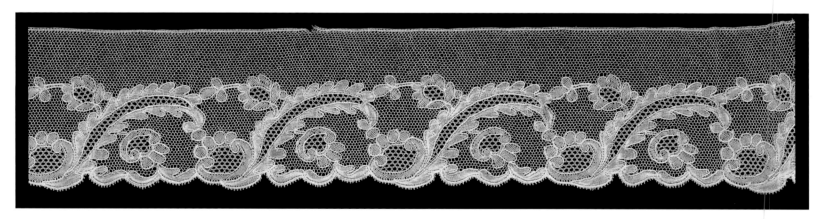

Plate 90
6408
Border; bobbin lace
Indian; 1850–70

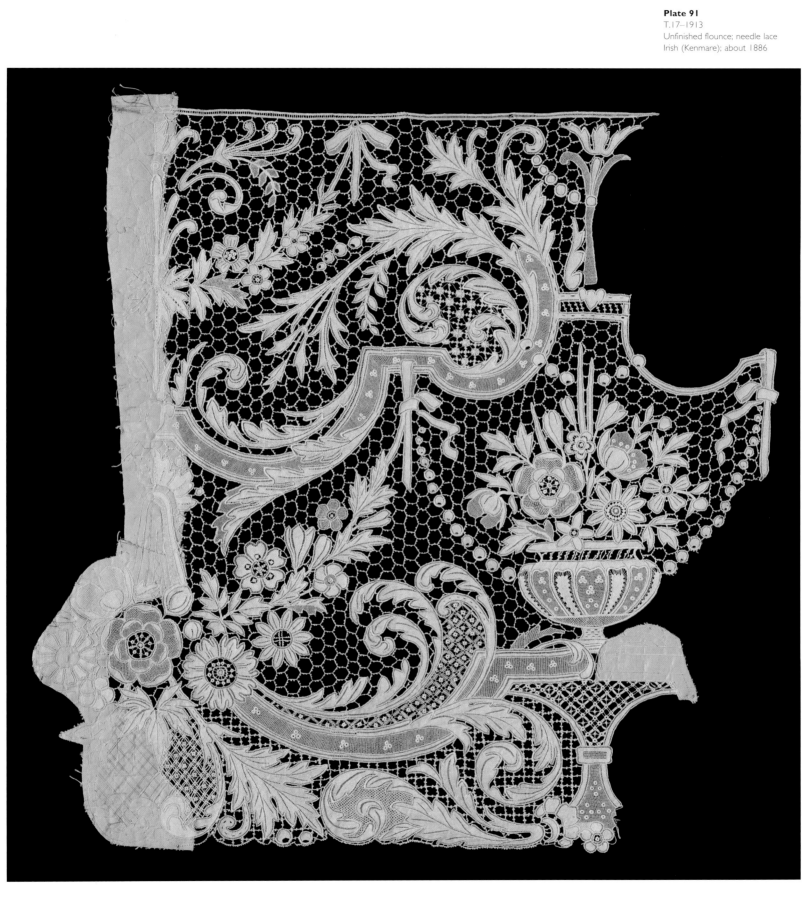

133

134

Plate 92
T.366–1970
Veil; needle lace
Belgian (Brussels);
about 1890

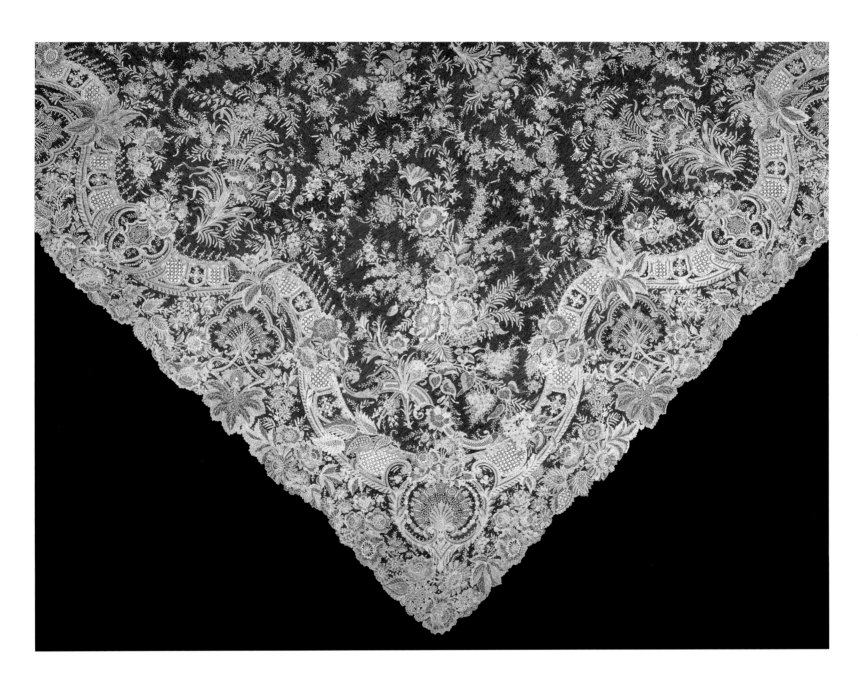

135

136   **Plate 93**
T.30—1965
Fan leaf; silk bobbin lace
French (Courseulles-sur-
Mer); about 1899

Plate 94
T.46&a–1951
Pair of flounces; bobbin and
needle lace
Belgian (Bruges or Brussels);
1900–10

137

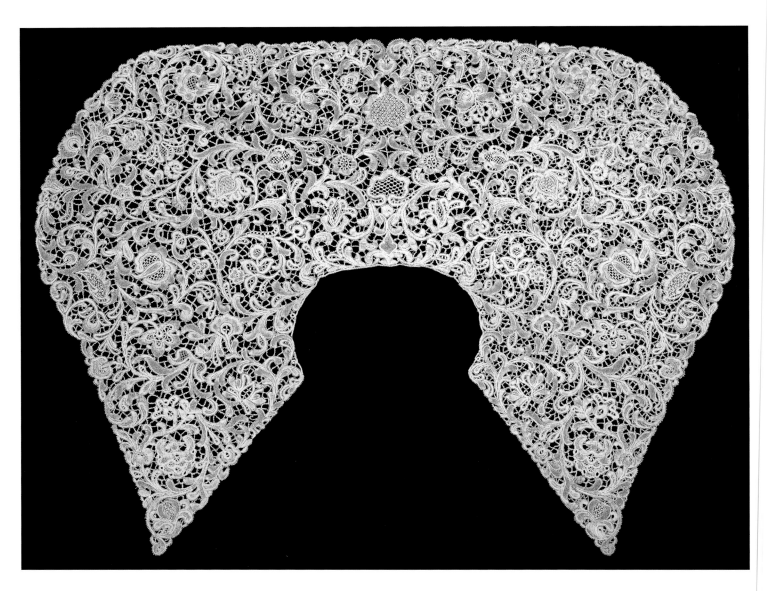

138

Plate 95
T.82–1946
Collar; bobbin lace
English (Honiton); about
1910

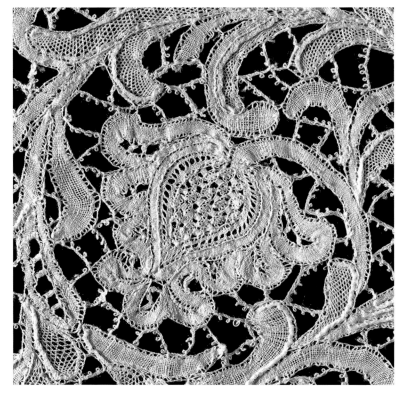

Plate 96
T.110–1936
Fan leaf; bobbin lace
English (Honiton); 1910

Plate 97
T.202–1921
Panel; needle lace
Hungarian (Halas);
early 20th century

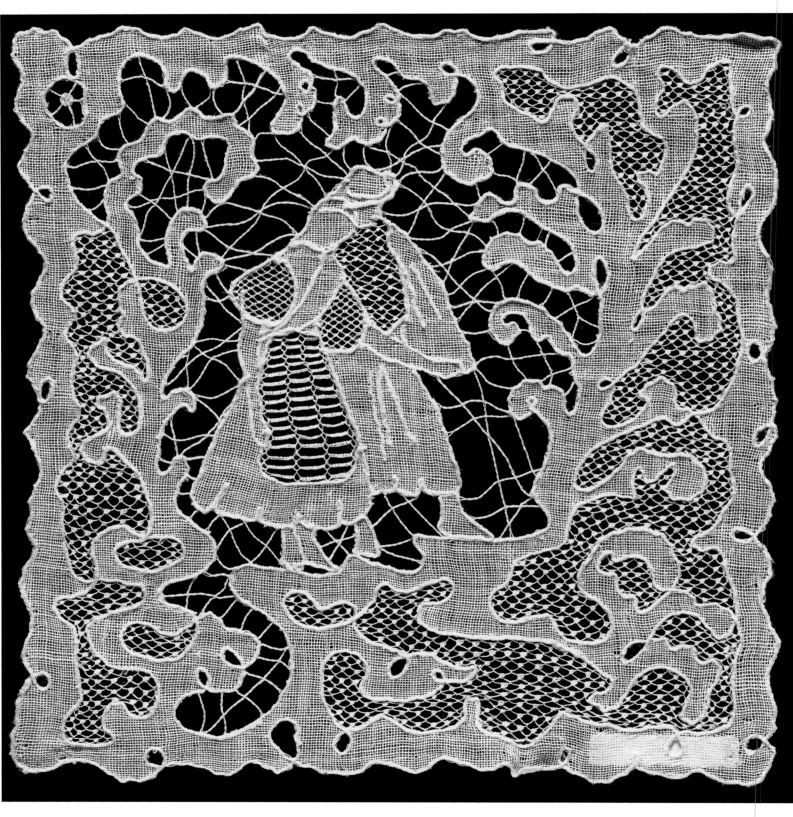

140

Plate 98
T.131–1986
Purse; cotton and
silk needle lace
English; 1986

141

Plate 99
T.85–B, H, J & K–1973
Samples; needle lace
Austrian; 1920s

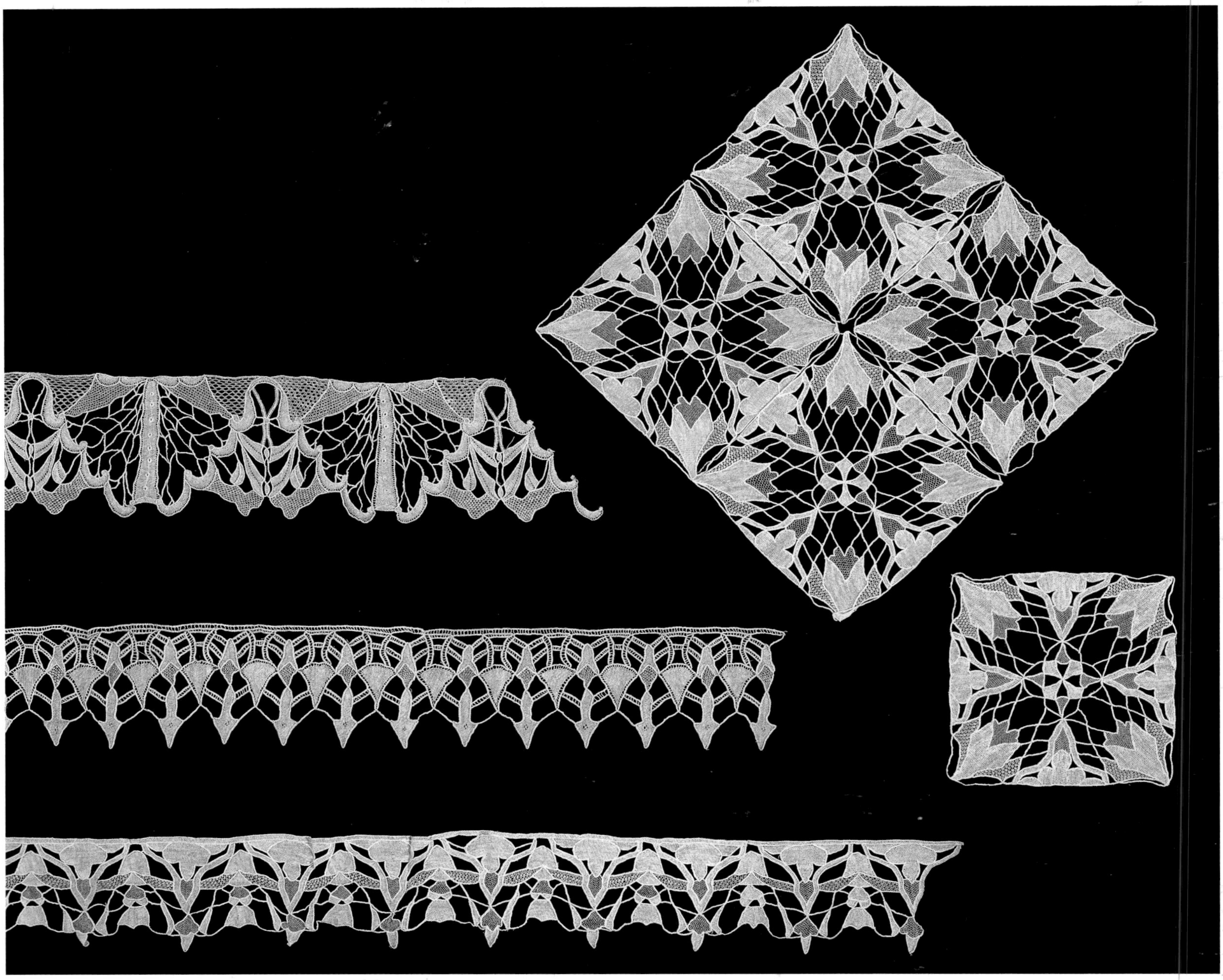

142

Plate 100
T.18–1979
Sampler; cutwork
and needle lace
English (Cumbria;
Ruskin Lace School);
1972–7

143